Gifts of GILEAD

Popular Insights

Solving the DaVinci Code Mystery
Brandon Gilvin

Wisdom from the Five People You Meet in Heaven
Brandon Gilvin and Heather Godsey

Unveiling the Secret Life of Bees
Amy Lignitz Harken

Gifts of GILEAD

AMY LIGNITZ HARKEN
LEE HULL MOSES

ST. LOUIS, MISSOURI

Cover art: Created from photograph by D. Jeanene Tiner
Cover and interior design: Elizabeth Wright

Visit Chalice Press on the World Wide Web at
www.chalicepress.com

10 9 8 7 6 5 4 3 2 1 05 06 07 08 09

Library of Congress Cataloging–in–Publication Data

Harken, Amy Lignitz.
Gifts of Gilead / Amy Lignitz Harken and Lee Hull Moses.
p. cm.
ISBN-13: 978-0-8272-3027-9 (pbk. : alk. paper)
ISBN-10: 0-8272-3027-3
1. Robinson, Marilynne. Gilead. 2. Christian fiction, American—History and criticism. 3. Kansas—In literature. 4. Clergy in literature. I. Moses, Lee Hull. II. Title.
PS3568.O3125G554 2005
813'.6—dc22

2005013293

Printed in the United States of America

CONTENTS

baseball unites _brother to brother
freind to frend

INTRODUCTION

Time, like an ever-rolling stream,
Bears all its sons away;
They fly forgotten as a dream
Dies at the opening day…

More than once these lines from Isaac Watts course through the mind of the Rev. John Ames III in *Gilead*, a novel by Marilynne Robinson. This eighteenth-century English hymn, "O God, Our Help in Ages Past," is based on Psalm 90, in which the psalmist considers the fleetingness of life on earth in light of the eternal nature of God.

Life on earth and life in paradise are very much on Ames's mind as he lives out his final weeks and months in the small fictional town of Gilead, Iowa, in the mid-1950s. As a man of faith, Ames believes that the hereafter, whatever it may be like, will be much sweeter than earthly life. Yet he finds life in Gilead has borne such a depth of sweetness and goodness, mystery, profound grace, and unimaginable blessing in the midst of sorrow that he cannot help wishing he could linger there a little longer.

The seventy-six-year-old Ames has been diagnosed with a heart condition and does not expect to live long enough to share his experiences, reflections on life, and family history with his seven-year-old son. So that the boy can know his father, Ames begins to write him a lengthy letter. In its pages, he shares family stories, great joys and deep sorrows, important journeys, significant relationships, and hope for the life to come.

Relationships between fathers and sons are at the crux of this novel. The Rev. John Ames himself is the son of a minister, the Rev. John Ames, and the grandson of a minister, the Rev. John Ames. Ames I (the grandfather) was an eccentric, passionate preacher who had visions of Jesus well into his old age. A staunch abolitionist and a Kansas Free Soiler, he preached in his little Civil War-era church with a pistol in his belt. Ames II, on the other hand, was a committed pacifist who couldn't stomach his father's fiery sermons or his beliefs about war. In reflecting upon their stormy relationship,

Ames III empathizes with both and offers his own reflections on family, friendship, and forgiveness.

Ames's letter-writing coincides with the return of Jack Boughton, one of the many "prodigal sons" in the novel. Baptized "John Ames Boughton," Jack is the wayward son of Ames's lifelong friend and colleague, a Presbyterian minister. Jack's homecoming opens up old wounds with which Ames is forced to come to terms before he can find peace.

Gilead is a small town, and John Ames III the pastor of just a small flock. Yet, his world is as broad as the concerns any minister faces: death, disbelief, grace, forgiveness, repentance, and reconciliation. His mind is as deep as the theologians and scripture that helped shape his thoughts; and his heart is as full as the love offered by a beloved wife, a cherished son, a lifelong friend, and a devoted congregation.

As the end of summer begins its approach, we shouldn't be surprised that Ames wonders whether he will live to see the end of the baseball season. The great American sport binds generation to generation, brother to brother, friend to friend, man to the world around him. And, in the end, these human connections are what occupy the aging minister as he prepares to say farewell to a good life.

Gilead is the story of a dying man, but it is not a story about death. We understand Ames's letter to his son as a celebration of life and all its gifts. As Ames reflects back over a long life, he finds blessing in sorrow and joy in mere existence. He struggles with questions of forgiveness and grace, regret and reconciliation. He remembers times gone by and lessons learned. He gives thanks for the many gifts of life.

We start our study guide by exploring the notion of storytelling in *Gilead*. The first chapter takes a look at some of the significant stories Ames tells his son. We examine the importance of storytelling in families and in society, as well as the role storytelling plays in the Bible.

In the second chapter, we look at the resources Ames leans on throughout his life. He is a well-educated man, having sent away for more books than he had time to read during his long years as a bachelor. He quotes scripture and theology with ease, drawing on each to inform and support his faith. We look at some of the many scriptural references in the novel, dig a little deeper into the theologians Ames relies on, and explore the other resources he utilizes in his life as a minister, husband, and father. In this chapter, we introduce the motif of the prodigal son, a significant theme throughout the novel and taken from Jesus' parable in Luke 15:11–32.

Prayer is central to John Ames's life and is the focus of chapter 3. Ames relies on these conversations with God to help him interpret and navigate the vagaries of life, including Jack's return to Gilead, his own feelings of anger and disappointment, his regrets, and his impending death. We look at Ames's prayer life, including his prayers for those around him and his prayer to find peace in his own life. By exploring Ames's prayers, we hope also to gain insight into Ames's own understanding of humanity's relationship with God.

Chapter 4 focuses on remembering. Here we look back on the historical setting of *Gilead,* following the Ames family through four generations. We return to the prodigal son theme and explore the complexities of relationships between fathers and sons, ending with a look at journeys taken and legacies left behind.

Chapter 5 examines the peculiarities of the life a minister leads. In addition to rigorous and deep thought about issues such as forgiveness and grace, Ames also lives with one foot in the day-to-day lives of his congregation. We look at Ames's sermon writing, clergy colleague, and the difficult questions parishioners pose to him. This chapter also explores the women of *Gilead,* suggesting how they provide ministries that the clergymen cannot, or will not.

Our final chapter helps us explore the many blessing moments in the novel, and those instances in which blessing is sought and found in the midst of hardship and despair. We also consider the baptisms and the eucharistic moments, as well as those moments in which God blesses an activity with beauty and wonderment. We conclude with Ames's final blessing of Jack Boughton, a blessing Ames had wished for, and was able, finally, to bestow.

Gilead is a joy to read. As we read through our favorite passages again and again, we find ourselves being wrapped up in Robinson's words, each sentence so grace-filled and meaningful that we could have written a whole chapter on each. Our hope is that this study guide will help you appreciate *Gilead,* and perhaps read it on a deeper level. We have tried to explain obscure scriptural references, provide basic background for theological issues raised, and refresh your memory about some of the historical events. There are three ministers with the same name in this novel, which makes talking about them somewhat cumbersome. For clarification, we refer to the grandfather (the Civil War chaplain) as Ames I. His son, the pacifist, is Ames II. The narrator is Ames III, but only at those points in which calling him simply "Ames" would be confusing.

We find ourselves returning again and again to certain scenes in the novel. We are especially drawn to the story of Ames I helping fugitive slaves, and the shouting match between Ames I and Ames II over preaching that had "*nothing* to do with Jesus" (*Gilead,* 85). We keep being called back to Rev. Boughton's front porch, where predestination is debated in the twilight, or to the bus station, where Jack receives Ames's final blessing.

Gilead is not a linear book; neither is our study guide. You will find that themes overlap and wend their way through our chapters. You will no doubt find topics and motifs that aren't mentioned here, such as the popularity of the pantry to hide forbidden things and behaviors, the peripheral but remarkable character of Soapy the cat, or (with the exception of Glory) the notable absence of daughters.

You are encouraged to explore these issues in a group or with a friend, asking yourselves how you find these ideas meaningful, and what the author might be trying to convey through them. If you're using this guide in a reading group and have the luxury of time, you might spend one session on each chapter. There is easily enough to discuss to warrant six sessions. We have incorporated biblical references throughout each chapter, so your discussions could also include Bible study and theological reflection.

We write as two ministers serving in urban centers in the twenty-first century. In some ways, we feel far removed from Ames's small-town ministry of half a century ago; on the other hand, we know what he means when he says, "When you do this sort of work, it seems to be Sunday all the time" (*Gilead,* 232). We've read a little Calvin, though we're sure that Rev. Ames could talk circles around us in a debate about predestination. As yet, we haven't been called on to fix anyone's plumbing, but we have eaten our share of gelatin salads and dubious casseroles.

We hope you will join us on this journey through *Gilead;* it is a journey that takes us across the Kansas prairie, through generations of baseball lovers, and deep into the failing heart of a faithful man who dearly loves his family. In *Gilead*, we celebrate this God-given gift of life.

CHAPTER 1

The Story of a Life

Since many have undertaken to set down an orderly account of the events that have been fulfilled among us, just as they were handed on to us by those who from the beginning were eyewitnesses and servants of the word, I too decided, after investigating everything carefully from the very first, to write an orderly account for you, most excellent Theophilus, so that you may know the truth concerning the things about which you have been instructed.

(Lk. 1:1–4)

I will tell you some more old stories. So much of what I know about those old days comes from the time my father and I spent wandering around together lost in Kansas…Once or twice I did sit down. I just sat there in the heat and the weeds with the grasshoppers flying around my head and watched him walk away, and he'd keep walking till he was almost out of my sight, which is a long way in Kansas. Then I'd go running to catch up…

But the pleasant thing was that when I did stay alongside him he would tell me remarkable things I'm pretty sure he would never have told me otherwise. If there was supper he'd tell stories to celebrate, and if there wasn't supper, he'd tell stories to make up for the lack of it.

(*Gilead*, 104–5)

Think back to the last time you were gathered around a holiday dinner table with friends or family. How long was it before somebody told a story?

"Remember when Dad was a kid and he forgot to get off the bus and Grandpa had to go chasing through downtown after it?"

"Then there was that time that…"

"Well, when I was growing up…"

"And what was that story Grandma used to tell?

We all, it seems, have a story to tell.

The author of the gospel of Luke had a story to tell—one that had been told by many before him, one that will be told by many after him. He told this story, he claimed, so that his dear friend Theophilus, or any lover of God, might know the truth. John Ames also had a story to tell, the story of his life, and he told it, like Luke, so that his dear young son might also know the truth.

> Your mother told you I'm writing your begats, and you seemed very pleased with the idea. Well, then. What should I record for you? I, John Ames, was born in the Year of Our Lord 1880 in the state of Kansas, the son of John Ames and Martha Turner Ames, grandson of John Ames and Margaret Todd Ames. At this writing I have lived seventy-six years…
>
> And what else should I tell you? (*Gilead,* 9)

And he proceeded to tell a story.

The record of a life cannot be told in lists of names and dates. Stories are the way we tell our lives. Stories tell us who we are and where we came from. We use stories to pass on our values and our history. Sometimes, the telling of the story is as important as the story itself; often, the story is told more for the sake of the teller than the hearer. Storytelling is essential to the novel *Gilead,* and so we start our discussion here, where all great novels start: with a story.

Story functions on many levels in this novel. We as readers—along with the boy when he is grown—are the hearers of one long story: the story of John Ames's life, which he records for his son. But on another level, there are stories in this novel that are told and retold, stories such as every family has. Some are stories Ames heard told by his father and grandfather, and passed on to his son. Others are stories of his own life—tales from childhood, stories of life in the church. Still others are stories in the making as Ames was writing: Jack Boughton's return home, for one.

Professional storyteller Jerre Roberts suggests three images to help us understand the role of a story: that of *container, connector,* and *mirror* (www.tejasstorytelling.com,"Storytelling as the Language of Faith"). As a container, our stories hold our most precious treasures—our history, our values and beliefs, our hopes and our dreams. Stories function as connectors when they link generation to generation, people to people. Stories passed down from our ancestors make the lives of those who have come before more understandable, more real. Stories connect us to those to whom we may not have any other connection than our shared experience of hearing the same story. As mirrors, stories reflect truths about ourselves. In the telling of a story, we are able to see clearly who we are and from whence we have come. Stories as mirrors also reflect our potential and our hopes and dreams for what we might become. As we begin to think about the stories of *Gilead,* you might consider how they function as containers, connectors, and mirrors.

Around a holiday dinner table, a story is repeated that everyone knows by heart, and another year is celebrated. A family tells the story of their immigration to the country, and family history is preserved. A grandmother tells a little girl stories of when she was young, and a different era comes alive in the girl's mind. A father tells his son stories of his late mother's life, and her spirit lives on with them. Two friends share stories of grief in their lives, and their friendship grows deeper as their wounds begin to heal.

Stories are the essence of our lives, in the living and the telling of them. John Ames knows he will not live to tell his son the stories of his life, and so he writes them down and passes them on.

"And What Else Should I Tell You?": Storytelling in *Gilead*

Even as he faced death with the confidence of faith, John Ames grieved the loss of this life on earth. "Oh, I will miss the world!" he lamented (115). His life had been full of joys and sorrows, surprises, frustrations, and accomplishments. At the end of his life, reflecting on all that had happened, he began to tell the stories of his life. His stories told the history of his family and his community. His stories searched for meaning in trouble and in despair. His stories celebrated and gave thanks for the life he had lived. Through the telling of these stories, he ensured that his spirit would live on and he was given a taste of the eternal life in which he so faithfully believed.

The Horse in the Road: Stories as History

Ames was obviously not the first in his family to be a storyteller. He recounted stories not only of his own life, but of his father's life and grandfather's life as well. Like many storytellers, he adopted and adapted the stories of an older generation. He remembered the journey to Kansas in search of his grandfather's grave as a time when his father told him stories. Walking along the dusty road, thirsty and tired and hungry and sore, Ames struggled to keep up with his father, knowing that if he did, he would hear the most remarkable stories. Ames, in turn, told his own son these stories, along with his own tales. The stories he told capture important events in the lives of three generations of the Ames family, as well as provide the historical context to their setting.

One such story is that of the journey itself. The trip to Kansas was obviously significant in the life of the young John Ames III—it drew him closer to his father, it tested his physical and emotional limits, and it gave him some closure to the mystery that was his grandfather. Such stories allow us in some small way to participate in an experience that happened generations ago. Ames's recounting of the experience of being at the grave of his grandfather when the sun was going down and the moon coming up, grants us—and his young son—access to a special moment between father and son. It was a moment that Ames III clearly treasured, and the story of that experience was a gift he gave to his son.

Ames also told his young son stories so that he would understand the historical context of the boy's grandfather's and great-grandfather's lives. The historical context of pre- and post-Civil War Kansas affected much of Ames I and Ames II's relationship, and so to truly understand that relationship, Ames knew that his son must also understand the dynamics of that time. The story of the horse that fell through the road is one such story. Interestingly, Robinson chooses to have Ames tell this story without comment; Ames merely prefaced it as a good story his grandfather used to tell. It could be interpreted as having no more meaning than a good joke, but in fact, it's fairly important in understanding the context of the time. This story tells something of the passion with which people embraced the cause of the Underground Railroad, and the sense of community that was built around that passion. (This historical backdrop is quite significant to *Gilead*, and will be explored in more detail in a later chapter.)

Actually, Ames's preface to the story is a good example of the way storytelling works. Ames began by saying, "Here is a story my grandfather and his friends used to tell, and chuckle over. I can't vouch for it entirely, since, talking among themselves the way they did, I doubt they'd have thought embellishing a story was quite the same thing as departing from the truth" (58). In other words, whether or not the details of this story are quite accurate is not as important as the truths the story conveys. Lots of well-intentioned people tried very hard to protect escaped slaves, and they went to great lengths to do so; sometimes the best laid plans—and tunnels—went astray.

War, Disease, and Fatherhood: Stories That Search for Meaning

Often the greatest stories—not the funniest, or the most entertaining, but often the most powerful—come from the greatest tragedies as we seek to find some good or some meaning in what has happened. Ancient Israelites told stories of defeat in battle in an attempt to understand why God had let them down. In the same way, we tell stories of the Holocaust, seeking to understand how such inhumanity could be allowed to happen. No doubt, people in Asia for generations will be telling stories of the 2004 tsunami as a way to find meaning in such tragedy and destruction.

Often, telling the story of tragedy or danger can help us gain perspective and see the situation in a new light. Of his time wandering lost through Kansas, Ames said, "Well, we spent a good many days on the edge of disaster, and we laughed about it for years. It was always the worst parts that made us laugh" (16). Likewise, Ames told the story of the church that had caught fire not as a tragedy, but as a time when the community came together to work with one another in a time of need. It became the occasion for the ashy-biscuit communion that was so meaningful for Ames: "I can't tell you what that day in the rain has meant to me. I can't tell myself what it has meant to me. But I know how many things it put altogether beyond question, for me" (96).

Sometimes the telling of a good story is as much to the benefit of the teller as to the hearer. The storytelling in *Gilead* was certainly for the young boy to find his place in the family and to learn about the father he would not know, but it was also for Ames's own sake. In one sense, Ames told these stories because he was trying to understand his father and his grandfather, their relationship to each other and to him. He acknowledged that this might be an impossible task—"A man can know his father, or his son, and there might still be nothing between them but loyalty and love and mutual incomprehension" (7)—but he undertook it all the same. The stories he told about his grandfather and father—from the soldier his grandfather shot to his father's anger at watching his grandfather preach in a bloody shirt with a pistol in his belt, from the horse who fell through the road to the story of coins hidden in the cornmeal—were all attempts to come to a better understanding of Ames I, a man he knew sometimes only through his father's eyes, and a better understanding of his own father.

In the same way, Ames told stories of the tragedies he had seen as a way to find meaning in what felt like despair. He told his father's and grandfather's stories of the Civil War and the aftermath of it, for example, as a way of further explaining their tumultuous relationship, but also as a way of looking for some reason or some meaning in such destruction. Likewise, he told stories about caring for families affected by the Spanish influenza in a struggle to understand and find hope in that despair. Ames told the story of the death of Louisa and Angeline in the hope that he would find some reconciliation to his loss.

One of the most pressing questions of the novel is how Ames was to make sense of his troubled relationship with Jack Boughton. The novel has three important stories about Jack Boughton: the story of the child Jack fathered many years ago to the shame and disappointment of his family, the unfolding story of Jack's return to *Gilead*, and the story Jack himself told of his new wife and child. Ames acknowledged his purposes in conveying these stories to his son: "You might wonder about my pastoral discretion, writing this all out. Well, on one hand it is the way I have of considering things. On the other hand, he is a man about whom you may never hear one good word, and I just don't know another way to let you see the beauty there is in him" (232).

For Ames, as for all storytellers, telling the story allowed for deeper understanding. It helped him come to terms with his anger for Jack, and helped him sort out how he felt so that he was finally able to have an honest talk with Jack. Hearing Jack's own story about his current dilemma gave Ames new insights about this man, just as he hoped would be the case for his son.

Living and Laughing: Stories That Celebrate Life

Some of the stories Ames told his son in the letter were simply stories that captured precious moments of life—not necessarily stories with some greater meaning, but stories that described small details so that the boy would have some idea of what his father's life was like. Ames told the story of the parishioner whose water faucets in her kitchen sink were reversed so that cold water came from the hot faucet and hot from the cold. In recounting this story, Ames shared with his son a bit of his role as a small-town minister, in which he was expected to know everything from predestination to plumbing. In closing this episode, Ames noted another important function of storytelling—sharing joy: "The story made your mother laugh, though, so my labors are repaid" (152).

Through stories like this one, Ames's son would come to know something of his father's life without actually knowing his father. Other stories Ames told brought people to life whom the boy never knew in flesh and blood. The character of Ames I came to life through the stories about the eye he lost in the war, his conversations with the Lord in the living room, and the trip to Des Moines to see Bud Fowler play baseball. His eccentricity—but also his generous heart—came through in the stories of his stealing clothes from clotheslines to give to the needy. Ames gave his mother life through story as well: her attempts to hide coins and valuables in the dry goods in the pantry so they might be spared from Ames I, her triumph when she finally stood up to him and kept her hidden treasures, her despair as she watched the chickens get loose and the laundry ruined in a sudden thunderstorm.

For much the same reason, Ames told his son the story of how he met and fell in love with Lila, the boy's mother. It would no doubt be important for the young boy to hear about the courtship between his parents given the age difference between them and the fact that the boy will have few memories of his father. Ames was also, however, careful to tell his son about his first wife, Louisa, and his daughter, Angeline. Although these people will likely feel like ancient history to the boy, they are an important part of his family—indeed, Angeline was his half-sister. Having Louisa and Angeline come to life in the boy's mind is key to his understanding of his father, and the long loneliness Ames endured.

Ames also wrote stories about the boy himself, or not really stories, as such, but rather a description of what was going on while Ames was writing: "You and Tobias are hopping around in the sprinkler" (63). When the boy is older, however, he will likely treasure these small bits of what life was like when he was young and his father alive: "You were almost late for school. We stood you on a chair and you ate toast and jam while your mother polished your shoes and I combed your hair" (8). That image will surely tickle the boy when he is old enough to appreciate it.

"The Church Smelled Like Horses": One Gilead Story

As we can see, *Gilead* has a number of significant stories. Now that we have discussed how these stories function in the novel, it might be helpful to take a closer look at one story in particular. On that important journey to Kansas in search of his grandfather's grave, Ames first heard the story of the soldier his grandfather shot while the Union Army chaplain helped an escaped slave to freedom (105–10). Ames and his father were spending the night in a barn, waiting for the dawn to come so that they could continue their journey. The sound of owls awakened them, which reminded Ames II of the time long ago when he was awakened by strange noises at night and discovered Ames I in cahoots with John Brown, helping a slave escape. While cleaning up after his father and his friends, Ames II encountered a lone soldier, who later ran into Ames I, who shot him and left him for dead.

On one hand, we might read this story as a history story. We certainly learn something about the historical context by hearing this story, and another era comes to life. Kansas before the Civil War was a dangerous place, and the dark of night was filled not with the peaceful walks and prayers of Ames III, but with violence and crime. No doubt this was part of the reason that Ames II told Ames III this story, and why Ames III recorded it for his son.

But there was another reason that generations of the Ames family told this story. It is key to understanding the relationship between Ames I and Ames II and the legacy they left their descendants. The details of the story provide us with insight into the character of the first two Ames preachers, and help set the stage for their later disagreements. "[Ames I] was never really a practical man again after that day, my father said." Ames III recalls (108), and we learn a lot about him from this story: he clearly believed strongly in abolitionism, and would stop at nothing to achieve that end. He saw the church as a place from which to launch social justice, and didn't seem to mind the juxtaposition of faith and violence. In fact, it was the very next week that he began to preach with a pistol tucked into his belt.

Ames II, on the other hand, valued peace and nonviolence. After discovering what had been going on in the church sanctuary, he hurried to clean up after his father and the wounded men. He wiped blood off the pew benches and washed away the droppings from the horses. He saw the church as holy ground, and wanted at all cost to avoid conflict there; his father's pistol-preaching deeply disturbed him. This also helps us understand his need to worship with the Quakers for a time after coming home from the Civil War. The relationship between father and son, however, is never cut and dried—even as he deplored what his father had done, Ames II was relieved every day that no one discovered the crime.

The setting for the telling of this story is notable as well. This was not a story to be told around the dinner table. This was a story for late nights in strange barns with owls hooting. This was not, in Ames II's opinion, a proud moment in the life of the Ames family, but it was a story that needed to be told.

From Patriarchs to Parables: Storytelling in the Bible

It is not surprising that John Ames turned to storytelling as he reflected on his life; he is a man of deep faith and knowledge of scripture. As Jerre Roberts writes, "Story is the language of faith. All major religions communicate through story. We find their core belief, their wisdom, not in carefully formulated creed and cannons and laws, but in their foundational stories" (www.tejasstorytelling.com). Indeed, stories give life and substance to our faith. Bible stories are the first things we teach our children in Sunday school; the story of Abraham and Isaac, the story of the good Samaritan, and the story of the women at the empty tomb remain with us. These stories carry the meaning and value of a faith tradition. Ames knows these stories well, and assumes his son will also. Many of the stories Ames tells have biblical connections, and in the next chapter we will further explore the use of scripture in *Gilead.* Here, though, we will consider the importance of storytelling in the Bible.

In the Hebrew Scriptures and the Christian New Testament, stories are told often, and for a variety of purposes. From the patriarchs of the Torah to the parables of Jesus, people of ancient times told stories to communicate their faith and their tradition, passing on stories orally from generation to generation. They told stories to explain the origins of life and the identity of a nation, to carry on tradition and struggle with life's toughest questions. No doubt the stories evolved as they were told, adapting to fit time and circumstance, until they were canonized into the form with which we are now familiar. Of course, through many translations and our own interpretations, they continue to mean different things in different times and contexts.

An interesting parallel to *Gilead* is that Ames's son was to receive his father's stories in their written form, in the letter Ames wrote as he was dying. The stories that Ames heard orally from his father and his grandfather were committed to paper, which would ultimately change them. It is worth considering what the boy would lose by not hearing his father's stories aloud, as well as what he would gain by having such a precious keepsake.

Origins of a People: Stories in the Old Testament

The Bible contains stories that attempt to explain the existence of humanity. Whether God created humanity on the sixth day, or "when no plant of the field was yet in the earth" (Gen. 2:5), the stories of Genesis 1 and 2 describe the origins of life. With God in the role of Creator, these stories set the stage for the ongoing relationship between God and humans throughout the Bible. The story of Noah and the flood furthers this relationship, bringing to life the origin of the covenant that ties the people to God and God to the people.

The stories of the patriarchs—Abraham, Isaac, and Jacob, to name the primary players—are another sort of story. Descendants of the patriarchs most likely told these ancient stories orally, around campfires, passing them on from parents to children as a way of carrying on a tradition. They told the story of the origin of the community of God's chosen people. God said to Abraham, the first of the patriarchs, "I will establish my covenant between me and you, and your offspring after you throughout their generations, for an everlasting covenant, to be God to you and to your offspring after you" (Gen. 17:7). The stories that follow in the scriptures are the stories of this nation that grows from Abraham, and they are an attempt to understand and live into the covenant between God and God's people. Can you see similarities here between the stories Ames III told his son about Ames I, the patriarch of their family?

The story of the exodus from Egypt is perhaps the most pivotal of the stories in the Hebrew tradition. Through the leadership of Moses, God led the people out of slavery in Egypt, away from the hands of Pharaoh, through the desert wilderness and into the promised land. This story is told for its importance in the formation of the Israelite people. This significant story, in which the people called out to God to help them and God responded, defines the identity of the whole nation of Israel as the chosen people of God.

Other stories in the Hebrew Scriptures attempt to search for meaning in either triumph or defeat. The people of Israel told stories of victory in battle or political success to demonstrate that God watched over them and gave them strength. They told stories of tragedy, defeat, and oppression as a warning—the people must have sinned against God so that God's wrath was brought upon them; only repentance would redeem them in the eyes of the Lord. This search for meaning plays out in individual lives as well; generation upon generation has told the story of Job in an attempt to understand why a loving God allows such misery.

It is important to note that for much of Israel's history, the nation and its people were under siege or captivity from neighboring armies; this, no doubt, affected the way the Hebrew people told their stories. Most history is written by the winners—those who do the conquering—rather than those who are conquered. Here, however, the losers wrote the history. This lends all the more significance to the Hebrew Scriptures: The stories demonstrate the writers' deep commitment to a faithful God who heard their cries and never abandoned them. We are reminded that the point of view of the storyteller is important in understanding the story. As you read and explore the stories of *Gilead*, you might want to take note of how the point of view affects each story.

"Go and Do Likewise": Stories in the Christian Scriptures

The stories of the Christian New Testament are somewhat different in character. The gospels, of course, are full of stories Jesus told to his followers, most in the form of parables. Jesus used parables to convey to his audience his message in terms they could understand. Parables are actually metaphors or similes in story form. Utilizing common, everyday images and characters—trees, seeds, farmers, laborers—parables give hearers (or readers) a recognizable entry into the discussion. In this way, parables are a good example of how important stories are—they make the abstract concrete. The abstract concept of justice, for example, becomes concrete in the story of the laborers in the vineyard (Mt. 20:1–15). The abstract concept of loving one's neighbor comes alive in the story of the good Samaritan (Lk. 10:25–37).

A further characteristic of parables is that they are designed to shock or startle the reader into thinking differently about the story. The story of the laborers in the vineyard, in which each worker is paid the same amount regardless of how long he worked, invites us to reflect on what is meant by justice in the kingdom of God. Likewise, while the priest and the Levite walk by, the character of the good Samaritan who helps the injured man challenges assumptions about what is "clean" and who is "neighbor." Jesus told these parables, then, not so much to carry on a tradition or to convey an identity, as the stories of the Hebrew Scriptures do, but to teach a new way of understanding humanity's relationship to the Divine. Perhaps we can see examples of parables—stories that teach—in *Gilead*. Certainly Ames had something to tell his son about love and about justice. Is the story of Jack Boughton a parable about forgiveness?

After the death and resurrection of Jesus, the early church told stories to advance the growth of the church. In much the same way that Ames told stories about his mother, father, and grandfather to his son who did not know them, the gospel writers related stories about Jesus so that later readers could know something about his life. In the story of Jesus' weeping at the tomb of Lazarus, for example, we see his humanity; in the story of the healing of the lepers, we see his compassion. Jesus the man comes to life through the stories told about him. The book of Acts records stories of the martyrdom of Stephen and others, as well as the missionary journeys of Paul, to celebrate and remember the early days of the movement. The epistles tell the story of Jesus' life, death, and resurrection as a way to pass on this new tradition, to convey new understandings, and to proselytize to the unbelievers in an attempt to win new converts to the faith.

Just as the exodus is the pivotal story in the Hebrew tradition, the story of Jesus' resurrection from the dead is the most significant story in the Christian tradition. To Christians, the story of the empty tomb contains the truth of the Christian faith and the good news of God's triumph over death. John Ames knew the resurrection story well, and he believed in it deeply. As he looked forward to his own death, he wrote this letter to his young son in an attempt to discover how his own story fit into the story of the Christian faith.

The Stories We Tell

Life is fleeting, as John Ames well knew. The tome John Ames wrote to his son, knowing that he would not be around to tell the stories that had been meaningful in his life, was certainly a gift, a way to share in the ongoing story of the boy's life. But in the stories recorded, a bit of Ames lived on. Though Ames I and II were gone as Ames III wrote, they lived on through the stories and memories of Ames III. So would his son carry on the spirit of Ames III.

In closing, we might consider where we as readers fit into this important work of storytelling in *Gilead*. We are not, obviously, a part of the Ames family, and so the stories he told are not our stories. Or are they? Perhaps this is what happens in a good novel—the story becomes *our* story. Robinson allows us access to the stories of another family, and we see ourselves there. Ames's stories become our stories. We hear our own truths in his words. Was this not what happened to Ames himself when he read *The Trail of the Lonesome Pine*? He saw himself and Lila reflected, and it spoke to him: "It strikes me that your mother could not have said a more heartening word to me by any other means than she did by loving that unremarkable book so much that I noticed and read it, too. That was providence telling me what she could not have told me" (133).

Ames reminds us, then, to listen for the stories in our lives. Where do we see ourselves reflected? What stories do we tell that hold our history, our values, our dreams? How do we find meaning in sadness and celebration in joy? We are not, perhaps, all that far removed from the ancient Israelites who gathered under the stars to tell the stories of their ancestors, for we, too, discover our faith and pass on our traditions through the stories we tell. In the words of stories—our own, or another's—we seek, and often find, the truths of our lives.

QUESTIONS FOR DISCUSSION

1. How do you think the young boy will tell his family stories when he has children of his own? How will he portray his father and grandfather? How will he tell the story of the soldier Ames I shot?
2. What role does truth play in storytelling? Must a story be factual to have meaning? What does it mean to be "true"?
3. How do the stories of *Gilead* function as a connecter, a container, or a mirror?
4. What stories are important in your family? What meaning do they convey?
5. What are the most significant stories in your faith tradition? What truths do they hold? How do the stories of your life fit into the stories of your faith tradition?

For Further Reading

Madeline L'Engle, *Rock That Is Higher: Story and Truth.* Colorado Springs: Waterbrook Press, 2002.

Yann Martel, *Life of Pi.* New York: Harcourt, 2001.

Jane McAvoy, ed., *Kitchen Talk: Sharing Our Stories of Faith.* St Louis: Chalice Press, 2003.

Daniel Wallace, *Big Fish.* Chapel Hill: Algonquin Books, 1998.

Anne Streaty Wimberly, *Soul Stories: African American Christian Education.* Nashville: Abingdon Press, 1994.

CHAPTER 2

Life as Learning, Life as Leaning

But as for you, continue in what you have learned and firmly believed, knowing from whom you learned it, and how from childhood you have known the sacred writings that are able to instruct you for salvation through faith in Christ Jesus.

(2 Tim. 3:14–15)

"When this old sanctuary is full of silence and prayer, every book Karl Barth ever will write would not be a feather in the scales against it from the point of view of profundity, and I would not believe in Barth's own authenticity if I did not also believe he would know and recognize the truth of that, and honor it, too."

(*Gilead*, 173)

The Rev. John Ames III believed that in those bleak years before Lila entered his life, he was "just getting by on books and baseball and fried-egg sandwiches" (54).

Ames's life may have seemed pale compared to the life and love he would come to know, but his bleak assessment isn't quite accurate. Ames was also "getting by" on food the women of a caring congregation provided, on a deep and abiding friendship with a clergy colleague, on childhood memories, and on insights gained from the world around him. During that period of loneliness, Ames was also getting by on prayer, scripture, and faith.

In the previous chapter, we looked at the value of stories: hearing the stories of others and learning to tell our own stories from the raw materials of experience. From the time we enter the world, we are exposed to people, ideas, and customs. We gain skills, make friends, and have adventures. We hear family histories, create memories, read books, and learn a moral code. In times of pain, transition, or confusion, we may draw upon any of these to help us get by. A woman tempted to have an extramarital affair might recall her wedding day. A teenager facing peer pressure looks at his "WWJD" bracelet. A man facing hip surgery leans upon a good friend for support and advice. A new widow turns to a book about grief. In a sense, life is learning, then leaning.

In this chapter we'll look at the resources on which Ames and others draw in the novel. As Robinson makes ample use of scripture, we'll spend considerable time examining Bible references. We'll look more briefly at some of the primary theologians she cites and also consider some of the other resources in the novel.

Ames's grandfather, father, and brother left Gilead, Iowa, because the little town could not satisfy their needs. But Gilead provided Ames with a wealth of resources to sustain him through years of sorrow, hardship, and, finally, joy.

Faith of Our Fathers

At a recent funeral, a grown man stood at the pulpit, tearfully recalling the many things he had learned from the father who lay in the casket before him. "He taught me not to be afraid of hard work," the son said. "He taught me to take care of my car. He taught me that a man takes care of the people he loves. He taught me that a real man does housework..."

In recounting those things a boy learns at the feet of a father, the unnamed son of the Rev. John Ames III would have only a small opportunity, were it not for the lengthy letter his father left. As we consider learning tools in *Gilead*, we recognize that the entire text is intended to be a learning tool. Ames wanted to pass along to the boy not simple accounts of family history, but also the wounds, the regrets, the celebrations, and the ambiguities of human love. He wrapped the accounts in scripture and theology, so that his son might not only know dates, names, and places, but also might come to know his father's faith and beliefs. Ames hoped his boy would benefit from his reflections on his experiences: "If I had lived, you'd have learned from my example, bad as well as good. So I want to tell you where I have failed, if the failures were important enough to have had real consequences" (134).

Ames peppered the account of his life with fatherly advice on subjects ranging from dealing with insult to faith and prayer: "There are pleasures to be found where you would never look for them. That's a bit of fatherly wisdom, but it's also the Lord's truth, and a thing I know from my own long experience" (39).

Given the stormy father-son relationships in *Gilead*, we are not surprised that Ames wanted to leave his son this lengthy letter. What a luxury such a letter would have been from his father; how beneficial an account written by Ames's grandfather (Ames I) would have been to Ames's father (Ames II). As it was, each man was left to interpret actions and words, sometimes spoken in anger, through a veil of bitterness, resentment, and disappointment. Ames recalled the betrayal he felt when his father moved from Gilead: "My father threw me back on myself, and on the Lord. That's a fact, so I find little to regret. It cost me a good deal of sorrow, but I learned from it" (236).

Life experience is an invaluable resource, to ministers just as it is to everyone. In subsequent chapters, we'll look more closely at the relationships and experiences of Ames and the other *Gilead* characters. In this chapter we'll focus on the formal learning.

The "Four-Legged Stool"

Sitting on the porch of the Boughton home, Jack asked Rev. Ames about his views on the doctrine of "predestination," the idea that God has predetermined who will be saved. The reactions to this question by Ames and Glory, Jack's sister, indicated that this was a very sticky subject, and a sore topic.

Anyone who thinks about God, or some concept of a higher divinity, is, in a sense, a theologian. We all have ideas about the existence and nature of God and about the relationship between God and us human beings. How do you sort out your feelings on complicated questions related to God? Anglican theologians are often credited with the idea of a "four-legged stool." In this concept, we have four resources on which we can lean: Tradition, Scripture, Experience, and Reason. We hold these four "legs" in balance to help us sort through an issue.

As he sat on Boughton's porch faced with that question, Ames drew on the four "legs." First, he appealed to tradition, what previous generations of Christians had believed: "there are certain attributes our faith assigns to God." As the elder Boughton joined in the conversation, he also appealed to tradition: "I hope the Presbyterian Church is as good a place as any to learn the blessed truths of the faith, including redemption and salvation first of all."

Next, Ames appealed to scripture: "I don't believe a person can be good in any meaningful sense and also be consigned to perdition. Nor do I believe that a person who is sinful in any sense is necessarily consigned to perdition. Scripture clearly says otherwise in both cases" (151). Yet one sentence later, Ames admitted that scripture wasn't clear on every point.

Jack then asked Ames to draw on his experience, and Ames described the consistency between a person's nature and his behavior. And reason? The very question of predestination, it would seem, defies the limitations of human reason: "there are things I don't understand" (152). To end the debate, Ames recommended that Jack read the writings of theologian Karl Barth.

For the characters involved, the conversation ended in frustration. For readers, it may seem as if Ames was being coy in answering the question or trying to skirt the issue of predestination altogether. Perhaps the tension in this scene lies with Ames's attempt to reconcile the four "legs." Many people who give careful consideration to their belief system find difficulty in reconciling some parts of it with others. Sometimes our own experience does not jibe with what our religious tradition dictates; sometimes a passage of scripture doesn't seem very reasonable. Sometimes portions of our faith tradition don't seem to square with what we understand the Bible to say. Yet ignoring one or more "legs" without first giving them due consideration is depriving ourselves of a rich encounter with God. Each person must decide how to hold the four "legs" in balance. The model is useful for non-Christians as well. While for them scripture may not be a suitable "leg," they may well turn to writings, tenets, and collections of histories and witness by forbearers in the faith of other religions. The important thing is that we can rely on more than just our own experience, or just the experience of others. According to the four-legged stool model, resources for thinking through quandaries come both from within our own being (reason and experience), and from outside ourselves (writings, testimonies, and traditions).

The "Legs" of Reason and Tradition

To help sort out questions of faith, some people turn to theologians who have wrestled with these problems over the centuries. Sometimes theologians are so influential that their views become part of a faith tradition. Lutherans ascribe much of their tradition to the thinking of Martin Luther; Disciples of Christ attribute some of their theology to the reflections of Barton Stone and Alexander Campbell. Catholics have a rich history of reason and tradition dating back to the first generation of Christian thinkers.

Below is a thumbnail sketch of the more prominent theologians Ames cited, specifically regarding the issue of predestination, although their writings cover a breadth of topics.

Augustine (354–430, from what is now Algeria) was one of the first theologians to grapple with the notion of predestination. According to Augustine, because of Adam's disobedience to God in the Garden of Eden ("the fall"), all humanity is oriented to sin and doomed to eternal death. We love ourselves more than God, and we seek satisfaction in material things. Our orientation to sin dooms us in a number of ways. First, while we have "free will," we cannot use it for the good without God's help. Second, not everybody can accept the help (grace) that God offers. God has chosen some people, however, to receive a special portion of divine grace that enables them to accept God's help. In other words, God gives grace to everybody, but to only some does God give the grace to accept it. Those will be saved.

John Calvin (French, 1509–64), one of the most influential contributors to the Protestant Reformation, was greatly influenced by Augustine. Like Augustine, Calvin believed that the fall corrupted human nature. But according to Calvin, not only does God determine who will be saved, but God also determines specifically who will be damned. This is known as "double predestination." Calvin was very interested in church order and church discipline, and also believed that secular government should set God's glory as its goal. "Calvinism" is the school of thought that developed during and after Calvin's lifetime and was heavily, but not exclusively, influenced by him. In England, Calvinism produced Puritanism, which in America became Congregationalism (Ames's tradition). Calvinism also produced Presbyterianism (Boughton's tradition).

Karl Barth (Swiss, 1886–1968), like many of his generation, was greatly influenced by the horrors of World War I and the impending second World War. World War I destroyed a confidence in humankind's achievements in reason and technology. (Note Ames's feelings about the war.) Barth came to oppose the prevalent liberal theology that emphasized reason, feeling, culture, and experience. He felt this was a sinful attempt to blur the infinite qualitative difference between God and humankind. The fall, Barth believed, tainted not just humanity's ability to do good, but humanity's ability to reason. He argued that Calvin's interpretation of predestination was not biblical. According to Barth, the whole point of Christianity is that, in the incarnation of Jesus Christ, God shows that God is "for man." The idea that God is secretly withholding salvation from some people is theologically impossible.

Ludwig Andreas Feuerbach (German philosopher, 1804–1872) was a student of the influential Christian philosopher Georg Wilhelm Friedrich Hegel. Feuerbach believed that our human struggles with goodness and badness in earthly life are transcended in a more ultimate sense of life and that our human limitations are overcome by the infinite. Ames touched on this when he talked about "an embracing, incomprehensible reality" (238). Feuerbach grew openly hostile to Christianity and rejected all notions of transcendence. According to Feuerbach, all religion, including Christianity, is an illusion. As pessimistic as this might sound, remember what Ames said about Feuerbach:

> Feuerbach is a famous atheist, but he is about as good on the joyful aspects of religion as anybody, and he loves the world. Of course he thinks religion could just stand out of the way and let joy exist pure and undisguised. That is his one error, and it is significant. But he is marvelous on the subject of joy, and also on its religious expressions. (*Gilead,* 24)

Feuerbach wanted to restore the dignity of humanity's natural existence. He believed that religion should be about the substance of life, not just ideas. He believed that attributes such as love and wisdom are part of the human experience, but that religion has claimed them as belonging to God. In this way, the best parts of a person's humanity are made foreign to her or him. Feuerbach's teachings inspired the work of Freud and Marx, as well as many Christian thinkers. *The Essence of Christianity,* often cited in *Gilead,* is Feuerbach's best-known work.

We conclude this section on "Reason and Tradition" much as many theologians and preachers ultimately conclude their reflections on an almighty, omnipotent, omnipresent God. When talking about things ultimate, many times our human reason is eluded. As Ames wrote, "The Lord absolutely transcends any understanding I have of Him" (235).

The "Leg" of Scripture

During that trip across the barren Kansas prairie, some people would ask for Ames's father to "open a bit of Scripture" (16) for them. In times of life transition, crisis, joy, and celebration, scripture, or passages from the Bible, can give shape to experience. Scripture can express that which escapes our own ability to verbalize.

Scripture can help us make sense of life events. Words from the ancient texts can give temporal concerns the stamp of the eternal, bringing comfort, hope, and communion with the Almighty.

The Bible is the story of God, God's activity in the world, and God's interaction with human beings. It begins with the creation of the cosmos in the book of Genesis and tells the story of God's people, from Adam and Eve to Noah, from the patriarchs to Moses, from King David to the prophets. The New Testament tells the story of Jesus of Nazareth. It includes reflections of the earliest Christians. The Bible contains histories, poetry, letters, prophecy, and narratives. It was written by a variety of people over many centuries in a plethora of circumstances. War, human love and sexuality, kingly courts, murder, captivity, family stories, hope, doom, fear, and praise are all included.

Because of the breadth of topics and circumstances present in the Bible, scripture can express the gamut of human emotions. Psalm 137, written during a time of defeat and captivity, expresses despair and rage. In writing to the Roman Christians, Paul gave voice to his confusion and frustration over his own behavior (Rom. 7:15). The Bible can also be a source of instruction. Recall how Ames turned to the Bible to help him through his attraction to Lila. Ames, however, turned to a passage that reflected his anguish, rather than something that might solve it: "'I am sick with love.' That's Scripture. It makes me laugh to remember this—I turned to the Bible in my crisis, as I have always done. And the text I chose was the Song of Songs!" (207).

Ames's formal learning began in childhood with the memorization of Bible verses, and study continued throughout his life, as it did in the lives of all the *Gilead* ministers:

> And Scripture. I never knew it the way my father did, or his father. But I know it pretty well. I certainly should. When I was younger than you are now, my father would give me a penny every time I learned five verses so that I could repeat them without a mistake. And then he'd make a game of saying a verse, and I had to say the next one. We could go on and on like that, sometimes till we came to a genealogy or we just got tired. Sometimes we'd take roles: he'd be Moses and I'd be Pharaoh, he'd be the Pharisees and I'd be the Lord. That's how he was brought up, too, and it was a great help to me when I went to seminary. And through the whole of my life. (*Gilead,* 67)

The tradition of teaching scripture continued with Ames's son, who at the age of six knew the Lord's Prayer (Mt. 6:9–13), Psalm 23, and Psalm 100, and was learning the Beatitudes, the "Blessed are..." sayings that begin the Sermon on the Mount of Matthew's gospel, chapters 5—7.

The Languages of Scripture. Besides memorizing verses, the ministers also learned to study scriptures by learning the languages in which they were written: Hebrew and Greek. The Old Testament, or Hebrew Scriptures, was written mostly in Hebrew, with a little Aramaic. The New Testament, or the Christian Testament, was written in Greek. Our English versions of the Bible are translations from ancient manuscripts written in those languages. Many ministers seeking to understand a passage of scripture study it in its original language. These ministers find that the process of translation into English can strip a passage of its subtlety or sacrifice a crucial nuance of meaning. Sometimes translations fail to recognize wordplays, rhyming schemes, and language rhythms. These syntactical issues can contribute to the meaning of scriptures. Studying scripture in the original Hebrew or Greek can help a minister understand the message the writer was attempting to convey.

Many seminaries require ministerial students to study Greek or Hebrew or both. Some denominations, including Presbyterianism, require ministers to have a working knowledge of both languages. Boughton and Ames relied on their language skills throughout their ministries: "I even kept up my Greek and Hebrew pretty well. Boughton and I used to go through the texts we were going to preach on, word by word" (65).

Language and Lens. Scripture can provide a language and frame of reference for our experiences. In fact, scripture almost served as a "second language" for the Gilead ministers as they used imagery and verse to view and interpret the world in which they lived, and to express themselves. The Spanish influenza had the dimension of a biblical plague (42) (see Ex. 6—12). The rift between Ames's father and grandfather was like the story of Cain and Abel (82) (see Gen. 4:1–16).

For Ames, being able to dip into the world of scripture provided both comfort and guidance. In recalling the death of his infant daughter, Ames quoted Matthew 18:10: "Their angels in Heaven always see the face of my Father in Heaven" (*Gilead,* 56). Ames continued: "Many, many people have found comfort in that verse" (56). In thinking through whether Jack can change his ways,

Ames balanced his experience with scripture: "those who are dishonorable never really repent and never really reform. Now, I may be wrong here. No such distinction occurs in Scripture" (156–57).

The Bible also provides colorful stories that help us illustrate our own feelings. Awakened by Jack in the sanctuary, Ames crankily compared himself to Samuel's ghost being conjured by an embattled King Saul (167) (see 1 Sam. 28). In referring to the long legacies of ministers in his family, Ames said, "if my grandfather did throw his mantle over me, so to speak, he did it long before I came into this world" (204). In 1 Kings 19:19, Elijah put his mantle over Elisha, to signify his succeeding him as prophet for Israel. Ames's father called their trip across Kansas their "desert wanderings"(16), referring to the forty-year journey of the Hebrew people through the wilderness (Ex. 12—Deut.).

Even Ames's brother Edward, an atheist, quoted from scripture, citing 1 Corinthians 13:11 in refusing to give grace at the dinner table (26) and quoting the joyful Psalm 133 in playing baseball.

The pages of *Gilead* are packed with biblical references, and it would be unwieldy in this guide to review them all. However here are some of the more prominent ones:

Gilead. Gilead is the region just east of the Jordan River, in what is now the country of Jordan. You'll see many references to Gilead in the Old Testament, especially in the books of Joshua and Judges, which relate the history of the Hebrew people's occupation of Canaan. The region of Gilead roughly corresponds to the Ammonite kingdom; in Judges, the people of Israel frequently war with the Ammonites in Gilead. You may have heard of a "Balm in Gilead," which is the title of an old hymn. The phrase comes from Jeremiah 8:22, in a lament over Judah: "Is there no balm in Gilead? / Is there no physician there?" The balm could refer to resin from the Styrax tree of northern Gilead, widely used as medicine (see Gen. 37:25).

Twinkling of an Eye: In considering his transition from life to death, more than once Ames used the language of the apostle Paul.

> I'm about to put on imperishability. In an instant, in the twinkling of an eye. The twinkling of an eye. That is the most wonderful expression...While you read this, I am imperishable, somehow more alive than I have ever been...I want your dear perishable self to live long and to love this poor perishable world.(*Gilead,* 53)

In 1 Corinthians, Paul addressed a group of Christians wondering whether they would experience the same bodily resurrection as Jesus. Note the similarity in language of Ames and Paul:

> Listen, I will tell you a mystery! We will not all die, but we will all be changed, in a moment, in the twinkling of an eye, at the last trumpet. For the trumpet will sound, and the dead will be raised imperishable, and we will be changed. For this perishable body must put on imperishability, and this mortal body must put on immortality. When this perishable body puts on imperishability, and this mortal body puts on immortality, then the saying that is written will be fulfilled:
>
> > "Death has been swallowed up in victory. / Where, O death, is your victory? / Where, O death, is your sting?" (1 Cor. 15:51–55)

Bread of Affliction: The phrase comes from Deuteronomy 16:3, when the law is laid down for the keeping of the Passover. God told Israel to eat only unleavened bread, or "bread of affliction," in this annual spring festival. In this way, they would remember God's deliverance of the Hebrew people from slavery in Egypt; the people left with such haste they had no time for the bread to rise. Ames recalled the phrase when his father gave him a piece of ashy biscuit (95f.) Referring to the eucharistic biscuit as "bread of affliction" was fitting, as Jesus, in instituting the Lord's supper, was celebrating a Passover meal.

Gethsemane: Gethsemane is the name of the garden where Jesus, sorrowful and troubled, went to pray before the authorities came to arrest him, leading to his being crucified (Mt. 26:36–46; Mk. 14:32–42). In the garden, Jesus prayed to God to remove the terrible fate that awaited him, but submitted himself to God's will. In talking about the universality of the Lord's supper, Ames referred to celebration of the Lord's supper as "a time with the Lord in Gethsemane that comes for everyone" (114). Ames also referred to Gethsemane in reflecting on being old and approaching death while his son is young: "The Lord wept in the Garden on that night He was betrayed…" (141). Finally, Ames wrote of his seeing the dying elder Boughton, after bidding Jack Boughton good-bye: "I knew if I woke him up he'd be back in Gethsemane. So I said to him in his sleep, I blessed that boy of yours for you" (244). These moments represent various facets of the Gethsemane episode. What does Gethsemane represent in each scene? Why might Ames, in rocking his infant son, sing a hymn about Gethsemane? (66).

You can tell a lot about the *Gilead* ministers by the scriptures toward which they gravitated and by their interpretations of those scriptures. Ames's grandfather (Ames I) "lacked patience for anything but the plainest interpretations of the starkest commandments" (31). Not only did he give to all who asked (Mt. 5:42; Lk. 6:30), he also labored for those who needed wood to be split or a roof repaired, either for free or for food, understanding it as a biblical edict. On the other hand, Ames II noted that in doing so much work for others who needed it, his father left his own family virtually fatherless. Moreover, his wife tempered the scriptural mandate to give to the needy with ensuring resources for her own family (33). While Ames I preached about the righteousness of war with a pistol in his belt (101), Ames II preferred to preach from a more pacifist stance. His favorite verse was from an anti-war passage of Isaiah, that garments of war shall be burned (80).

Prodigal and Patriarchs: Two Primary Scriptural Motifs

Traveling by foot with his father through drought-ridden Kansas, young John Ames recalled the story of a preacher who was so unconfident of his Hebrew, "he'd walk fifteen miles across open country in the dead of winter to settle a point…" (16). Ames recalled the story during that trip "because it seemed to me we were doing something very similar" (16). What was the biblical truth they were trying to settle? Was it a circuitous, faith-testing journey akin to the forty-year wanderings by the Hebrew people? Was it the repentance and return of a son to his father, like the parable of the prodigal son in Luke's gospel? Or was it a father's sacrifice of his son, like Abraham's binding of Isaac?

Robinson employs a number of scriptural motifs in *Gilead*. Perhaps the most prominent is the parable of the prodigal son. You might also recognize shades of stories from the Old Testament patriarchs. By recalling these passages of scripture, we can draw parallels between the biblical stories and the stories in the novel. For example, Lila compared Ames to the biblical Abraham, in that each became a father in old age (54).

Employing a motif involves more than matching novel character to biblical character. If we see that such a match occurs, we can then extrapolate further parallels, or at least consider whether additional parallels exist. Using the Abraham example again, Ames insisted he was *not* like Abraham because he didn't have an elderly wife with whom to share the experience. Yet he *was* like Abraham in that he believed all parents inevitably "send our children into the wilderness" (119). Reading through the lens of a motif enriches our reading experience, because it offers the possibility of a depth of insight.

The Prodigal Son

The prodigal son (Lk. 15:11–32) is one of Jesus' most well-known and beloved parables. It is really the story of two sons. The younger son asked his father for his share of his inheritance early, left home, and "squandered his property in dissolute living" (Lk. 15:13b). With his money spent, he took a job feeding pigs. Poor and hungry, he returned to his father, repentant and ready to live as a servant. His father embraced him and called for a celebration. The older brother, who worked for and obeyed his father, became angry and demanded an explanation. The father responded that all he had would belong to the older son, but the return of the brother was cause for rejoicing: "because this brother of yours was dead and has come to life; he was lost and has been found" (15:32).

In general, Luke's gospel emphasizes embracing the outcast person, as well as the acceptability before God of those society marginalizes—such as women, the poor, those with physical limitations, and the "lost." We might think of the "lost" as people considered sinners in Jesus' time (such as tax collectors) who are "found" when they repent and turn to God. In this parable, we might see the father as God and the younger son as a lost sinner who repented. God forgives, embraces, and celebrates the repentant sinner. But we might also identify with the older brother, who in some ways also felt estranged from his father, having "slaved" for him yet never having felt rewarded. We might associate that son with religious people who stick to the rules themselves, and disdain those who stray, repentant as those sinners might be. This parable would tell us that God also loves those religious stalwarts, and that the benefits of their constancy are not compromised by God's elation over repentant sinners. The parable, then, is aimed at both sinners and the righteous. You might also find lessons of reconciliation, forgiveness, repentance, responsibility, and leaving and coming home in this parable.

Reading *Gilead* through the lens of the parable of the prodigal son is an interesting and complex endeavor because of the many generational parallels. One of the more obvious parallels is the story of Jack and his father. As prodigal, Jack strayed from the family morality, left home, returned, and claimed to repent. Ames commented: "[Boughton] has some fine children, yet it always seemed that this was the one on whom he truly set his heart. The lost sheep, the lost coin. The prodigal son, not to put too fine a point on it" (73). Jack was also the godson of Ames. As "father" to Jack's prodigal, Ames might be expected to offer forgiveness. Indeed, the question of Ames's forgiveness of Jack creates much of the novel's tension. Do you think Ames forgave Jack? Do you think Jack truly repented?

Jack isn't the only prodigal. Consider Ames's older brother, Edward. He, too, left home, abandoned the family's moral code, and returned. Common sense would have us believe that John Ames III would be the favored son, as he took up ministry and toiled in the profession. Yet Edward seemed to be the favored son. Recall how Ames II attempted to understand him by reading the same books. Eventually, he followed Edward to the Gulf Coast to live, leaving his pulpit to his other son, a resentful John Ames III. "As I have told you, I myself was the good son, so to speak, the one who never left his father's house—even when his father did, a fact which surely puts my credentials beyond all challenge" (238).

The Biblical Patriarchs

Just as three generations of ministers inhabit *Gilead*, three generations of patriarchs inhabit the pages of Genesis 12—36: Abraham, Isaac, and Jacob, the forefathers and pioneers of the Jewish faith. Like the story of the prodigal son, the accounts of the patriarchs include many stories of fathers and sons, and elder and younger brothers.

God sent Abraham (known at first as "Abram") forth from his own country with his wife Sarah (Sarai). On several occasions, God promised Abraham land, children, and blessing. Impatient for a child, Sarah gave to Abraham her Egyptian maid, Hagar, who bore a son, Ishmael (16:15). As matriarch, Sarah legally could claim the child as her own. Eventually, Sarah too bore a son, Isaac (21:2). Unable to bear the thought of the other boy in the household, Sarah bid her husband to cast the maid and Ishmael into the wilderness (see Gen. 21:8–21). Not long afterward, God "tested" Abraham by asking him to sacrifice Isaac, now considered his "only" child (see Gen. 22). At the last minute, with Isaac bound for sacrifice and Abraham raising his knife, a ram suddenly appeared. Eventually, Isaac and Ishmael reunited to bury their father, Abraham (25:9).

God's blessing of Abraham's line continued through Isaac, whom some scholars perceive to be a "bridge" character between his more complex father and his more colorful sons. He is a relatively passive character, relying on a servant of his father to fetch him a wife, Rebekah. Rebekah became pregnant with twins, Esau and Jacob (25:21–26), who struggled with each other even in the womb. Esau was technically the older, but Jacob came to supplant him in the patriarchal line.

Jacob, the last of the three patriarchs, is known as a "trickster." Many of his stories are filled with deception and reversals, either on his part or on the part of someone else. Many of his stories also concern Esau. The brothers were very different: Esau was an outdoorsman, a hunter, and a farmer; Jacob was a quiet man who preferred the indoors. (25:27) Jacob was the more clever of the two. He capitalized on Esau's hunger and impatience to eat, outwitting him to obtain his birthright (25:29). Later, spurred on by Rebekah, Jacob used deception to obtain from Isaac the deathbed blessing that was due to his brother (see Gen. 27).

To save himself from his enraged brother, Jacob traveled to Haran, to his uncle Laban. He fell in love with Rachel, Laban's daughter, and toiled for seven years to win Rachel's hand, only to be tricked on his wedding day into marrying the older daughter, Leah. Jacob labored another seven years to win Rachel's hand. More trickery ensued when Jacob and Laban negotiated a settlement by which Jacob might leave Laban's employ. On his return home, Jacob sent all his family and servants and livestock before him and remained by himself by the Jabbok River. There, a "man" wrestled with Jacob all night. This "man" turned out to be a divine being and put Jacob's thigh out of joint. When Jacob insisted on a blessing, the being gave him a new name, "Israel."

In a scene reminiscent of the prodigal son, Jacob approached his older brother in fear and in supplication, but Esau ran to meet him, embracing him and weeping. Much like Isaac and Ishmael, the twins Jacob and Esau united again to bury their father, Isaac (Gen. 35:29).

The line continued through Joseph, Jacob's favorite son. Joseph returned to his father after many years; Ames referred to this return when he remarked that he wished Boughton "could be like ancient Jacob" (243; see Gen. 48:11).

The stories of the patriarchs are stories of brotherly rivalry and reconciliation, devotion to fathers, deception of fathers, and willingness to sacrifice offspring to serve God. Read in their entirety, we notice that God was obeyed most of the time, but not all the time. Each patriarch was accused of deception, yet each one carried God's blessing.

Among the motifs in *Gilead* is the idea of a father's sacrifice of his son. Ames remarked that Abraham was called "to sacrifice both his sons" (129). While God provided relief in each instance, these biblical texts are not altogether easy to swallow. Imagine Ishmael's sense of betrayal at being turned out of the protective, prosperous household with his mother into the harsh wilderness. Imagine Isaac's horror at seeing the knife raised above him.

Despite any shades of biblical praise for Abraham, many theologians and preachers cannot read this biblical episode and see Abraham as heroic or passing a test; their sympathies lie with the boy. Some even see Abraham as failing any "test." Do you draw parallels between such attempted "sacrifices" and Ames I's treatment of his son? Ames II's treatment of his son? We might compare each of the ministers to Jacob, who wrestled with a divine being and was left with a limp for the effort. Also, each of the patriarchs declared a preference for a specific son over another. This preferential treatment causes much strife, anger, resentment, and even murderous intent in the hearts of the "other" sons. Do we find such bitterness expressed in *Gilead*?

A final note on scripture: Ames declared that Abraham's dealings with his sons were "the only two instances in Scripture where a father is even apparently unkind to his child" (129). Ames apparently forgot about Abraham's nephew, Lot. Lot offered his two virgin daughters to placate the men of Sodom who demanded to "know" two strange visitors who sought shelter in his home (Gen. 19:8). Again, in Judges, a man who offered shelter to a Levite and his concubine offered his virgin daughter to satisfy a similar crowd. In the end, the concubine is sacrificed. Significantly, she had run away from the Levite, seeking protection in the house of her father, but to no avail. (Judg. 19). We might also recall Jephthah, a Gileadite, who sacrificed his daughter to comply with a battle vow he made to God (Judg. 11:29–40).

Culture, Community, Church: Other Resources for Life's Journey

When we think of "resources," we might think of a source of supply, such as a country's "natural resources." We might think of money or material wealth, such as a person's "financial resources." We might think of the means or ability by which to accomplish something, such as the emotional resources to overcome grief or mental resources to invest our own money. In each of these examples, a "resource" is something useful on which we can draw when we need it.

We have discussed some of the more formal resources in Gilead, such as scripture, the writings and thoughts of theologians, and religious tradition. But we remember that Ames wasn't just "getting by" on books, but on baseball as well. In his years as a single man, Ames listened to the scratchy, nighttime signal of his radio to hear the plays and used his imagination to fill in the rest. Baseball was a respite, and a means by which he could transcend the confines of his mind. Baseball also was a resource for the men of Gilead to communicate, linking Ames with his grandfather, his father, his older brother, and with his son. Baseball also joined Ames's young son with his older godson.

Among other expressions of culture, Ames relied on poets. He especially cites John Donne and George Herbert, two seventeenth-century "metaphysical" poets who were also ordained priests in the Church of England. The term "metaphysical" was first applied to them by their contemporaries in a pejorative way, but by the twentieth century, critics had come to admire the poets' skills and daring, especially in the way they used philosophical and theological concepts. John Donne (1572–1631) was born into a Roman Catholic family, but quietly abandoned Catholicism. He is known for both his love poetry and his religious poetry (see p. 77 in *Gilead*). Herbert's (see p. 111 in *Gilead*) most well-known work is *The Temple,* published in 1633, a collection of religious and church-related poems that are both intense and quiet.

Ames also used the lyrics of hymns in contemplating life. We recall his singing "Go to Dark Gethsemane" as he rocked his infant son, and his reflections on the hymns of Isaac Watts (1674–1748), especially "O God, Our Help in Ages Past." "Good old Isaac Watts. I've thought about that verse often. I have always wondered what relationship this present reality bears to an ultimate reality" (103).

Church, of course, provided a resource for the Ames family. The congregation provided the family with a place to live, as well as food and a living. But beyond the walls of the Congregationalist congregation that the Ames men served existed an entire Christian community, made up of Presbyterians, Baptists, Methodists, and Lutherans who could rely on each other in times of difficulty. When the Baptist church burned to the ground, the entire community showed up to put out the fire, sing hymns, salvage what was salvageable, and dine together: "All kinds of people came to help. It was like a camp meeting and a picnic" (94).

In the days after the Civil War, when Ames I's congregation had dwindled, he "opened all the windows that still would open, so they could hear the Methodists singing by the river, and…some of the women would join in if the song was 'The Old Rugged Cross' or 'Rock of Ages,' even in the middle of the sermon, and he'd just stop preaching and listen to them" (100). Recall, too, Ames's appreciation of the Baptist's' practice of immersion baptism. In the Congregationalist tradition, infants are baptized with a small amount of water on their foreheads. But Baptists practice full immersion baptisms, in which those old enough to make a confession of faith are completely submerged in water.

All of Life Can Be a Resource

We might take our cue from the Ames family that resources can be found outside the confines of our own traditions. Just as the much diminished Congregationalist congregation was inspired by the hymns of the Methodists, and just as Edward, an atheist, found scripture to be the perfect way to express his joy over playing baseball with his little brother, we can find resources all around us to help us get by. The teachings of Jesus Christ greatly influenced Mahatma Gandhi, a Hindu. The Rev. Martin Luther King Jr. found Gandhi's practice of nonviolent resistance informative to his own strategy in the civil rights movement. Many non-Christians find inspiration in the pages of the Christian Testament, while many Christians find that elements of other traditions flesh out their understanding of the world around them. In neither case is it necessary for the person to abandon their cherished faith.

Restricting our ideas of what are valid resources truncates our ability to find ways to see, imagine, and interpret the world around us. Recall Ames's grandfather's reliance on his visions of Jesus to fuel his passion for ministry. Because his visions were so vivid to him, he discounted the ways in which God's wisdom manifested itself to his sons:

> I believe that the old man did indeed have far too narrow an idea of what a vision might be. He may, so to speak, have been too dazzled by the great light of his experience to realize that an impressive sun shines on us all. Perhaps that is the one thing I wish to tell you. Sometimes the visionary aspect of any particular day comes to you in the memory of it, or it opens to you over time…I believe there are visions that come to us only in memory, in retrospect. (*Gilead*, 91)

For Ames, many resources revealed themselves over time: the meaning of scripture, the musings of theologians, and the value of experiences many years before. In the meantime, he found resources in things like writing, solitude, and conversation with his dear friend Boughton.

Not every person uses resources in the same way. Ames, his brother Edward, his father, and even Jack Boughton had access to the same resources. Yet each had a different understanding of God. The Ames ministers each balanced theological works with their own experiences and reflections; Jack could not believe, even though he tried to "crack the code" and sought faith; Edward abandoned faith altogether. Speaking of Edward, Ames wrote: "But the fact is that his mind came from one set of books as surely as mine has come from another set of books. But that can't be true. While I was at seminary, I read every book he had ever mentioned and every book I thought he might have read, if I could put my hand on it and it wasn't in German" (125).

Further, we can't always put stock in the resources we think might be most likely to help us. For example, Ames lacked the spiritual resources to forgive Jack: "I don't forgive him. I wouldn't know where to begin" (164). This was true despite his preaching on forgiveness, his understanding forgiveness to be a Christian mandate, and his knowledge of scripture and theology on the necessity of forgiveness. Then, Ames learned about Jack's secret family: a wife and child. This family was unacknowledged and inaccessible to Jack. In this Ames found common ground with his godson. Ames's first wife and first child were dead, and in some ways unacknowledged by those closest to him (65). Yet they remained dear in his heart. The painful memory of his lost family and the revelation of Jack's family prove to be the resources Ames needed to find a path to forgiveness.

We can always rest assured that God will provide us with the resources we need. They can come in the pages of a book, in a phone call to a dear friend, in a time spent in quiet meditation. Stories from our own families about resilience, resistance, courage, and even failure can be sources of inspiration and comfort. The resources we find around us to help us "get by" may not be what we expect, or even what we want. But if we open our minds to the infinite possibilities of God, we will begin to see resources in surprising and delightful places.

QUESTIONS FOR DISCUSSION

1. The Bible is used for instruction, for edification, for comfort, and for understanding. Have you found this true in your experience? How do you read the Bible? Why do you read the Bible?
2. Marilynne Robinson makes much use of scriptural references. Some may be very familiar to you, while others may not. How do the familiar ones affect your reading of *Gilead?* Can those that are unfamiliar add to your understanding? Do they detract?
3. Ames had much fatherly advice for his young son. Can a person learn from another person's experience?
4. Ames found resources to sustain him through life in ways that his brother and father did not. Why is this?
5. List the resources in your life. They may include people, books, or various communities to which you belong. What makes for a good, useful resource?

For Further Reading

Augustine, *Confessions*. Oxford: Oxford University Press, 1998.

Forrest Church, *Freedom from Fear: Finding the Courage to Act, Love, and Be*. New York: St. Martin's Press. 2004.

Jeffrey C. Geoghegan and Michael M. Homan, *The Bible for Dummies*. New York: Wiley, 2003.

Parker Palmer, *The Active Life: A Spirituality of Work, Creativity, and Caring*. San Francisco: Jossey-Bass, 1990.

CHAPTER 3

Life as Prayer

Rejoice always, pray without ceasing, give thanks in all circumstances; for this is the will of God in Christ Jesus for you.

(1 Thess. 5:16–18)

It was on the nights I didn't sleep at all and I didn't feel like reading that I'd walk through town at one or two o'clock. In the old days I could walk down every single street, past every house, in about an hour. I'd try to remember the people who lived in each one, and whatever I knew about them, which was often quite a lot, since many of the ones who weren't mine were Boughton's. And I'd pray for them. And I'd imagine peace they didn't expect and couldn't account for descending on their illness or their quarreling or their dreams. Then I'd go into the church and pray some more and wait for daylight.

(*Gilead*, 71)

Whether or not we consider ourselves "religious," whether or not we try to have an active prayer life, most likely we have all uttered some kind of prayer at some time or another.

"Please, let me find a parking place," we mutter when we are late for a meeting.

In moments of panic, we pray without thinking: "God help me!"

Or the constant prayers we breathe with every breath: "Lord, please keep my daughter safe."

Maybe you remember prayers from your childhood, saying grace before meals with everything from "God is great, God is good, let us thank God for this food," to the chanted "Rub-a-dub-dub.

Thanks for the grub. Yay God!" and "Good food, good meat, good God, let's eat!"

The notion of prayer brings a whole variety of images to mind: an ascetic praying in the desert, a priest saying prayers at mass, a group of women gathered for support and prayer, an old man kneeling at the grave of his wife, a family giving thanks before dinner. Or the image of a child who kneels beside her bed with hands folded, reciting, "God bless Mommy, God bless Daddy, God bless Teacher" while a needlepoint sampler hanging on the wall above offers another sort of prayer: "Now I lay me down to sleep, I pray the Lord my soul to keep. If I should die before I wake, I pray the Lord my soul to take."

Although this bedtime prayer is not one that John Ames offered in *Gilead*, it seems possible that it was on his mind. Ames often connected sleeping with praying, and he was frequently doing one or the other. He fell asleep in the church while praying and waiting for Jack to arrive. At times when he couldn't sleep, he prayed. "I do recommend prayer at such times, because often they mean something is in need of resolving" (168). At the end of a writing session, he noted, "Much more prayer is called for, clearly, but first I will take a nap" (125), and elsewhere: "Now I will pray. First I think I'll sleep. I'll try to sleep" (131). And as the book closes, in what we are to assume are his final words, "I'll pray, and then I'll sleep" (247), reversing the order of the previous two passages and suggesting that the last thing he did in this life was to offer a prayer.

This is not insignificant for a man who spent his life praying. It was part of his profession, of course, but it was also part of his personal life of faith. He consistently turned to God in times of joy and in times of sorrow. He turned to prayer when he was conflicted or in doubt, and his prayers were often filled with hope for the future. Prayer, for John Ames, was a practice he learned well, and it was a learning he continued to practice.

Like most children, Ames began to learn this practice of prayer by observing his father and grandfather. He watched as his grandfather spoke to the Lord in the living room or the backyard; he did not always understand these visions, but knew that even these were a type of prayer. On the trip to Kansas, his father (Ames II) never failed to say grace before a meal, even if the meal was only a dirty and stolen carrot. When they found the grandfather's grave, Ames II knelt in prayer there, a prayer from which Ames III gently roused him to watch the magnificence of the moon and sun aligning. Prayer is a practice Ames III hoped his own young son would carry on: "Be diligent in your prayers, old man," he advised (210).

In a sense, Ames's letter *is* a prayer. The letter, as a prayer, was offered in thanksgiving for the life he led and in awe of the love of his wife and child. In some ways the letter is a prayer of confession of the regrets he had, of the reconciliations that could not be reached, and of the doubts that lingered. In other ways, the letter is a prayer of hope for the future and a prayer of lament for the suffering he endured and witnessed. "For me writing has always felt like praying, even when I wasn't writing prayers, as I was often enough. You feel that you are with someone" (19).

In this chapter, we'll approach *Gilead* as the final prayer of John Ames. We'll take a look at how he prayed as he looked back on his life and looked toward the life he expected in heaven. Ames's prayers will also help us uncover some of what he believed about life, the nature of God, and a life after death. We'll take some time to explore the notion of prayer in the Bible and consider the meaning of this slippery term. Finally, we'll reflect on what John Ames can teach us about prayer in our own lives today.

The Prayers of John Ames

If we indeed understand Ames's entire letter as a form of prayer, we look at what he wrote in a new light. In these pages are prayers of thanksgiving for the joys of life and prayers of lament for deep sorrow, both personal and communal. We find here prayers of contemplation that allow for moments of doubt, and prayers of hope for the future, the earthly future of his congregation, his friends, and his family, and the eternal future that the life of faith affords.

Neither John Ames nor the Bible offers a precise rubric for how one ought to pray; indeed, Ames prayed in all variety of forms and circumstances. Still, on occasion, we find it helpful to consider a pattern or guide to follow when praying. One example is the acronym ACTS, which stands for *adoration, confession, thanksgiving,* and *supplication*. ACTS provides a pattern for prayer that helps us remember to express our adoration of God and God's creation, confess our sins and inadequacies, thank God for all we have been given, and present our petitions and requests before the Lord. This pattern also provides us with a helpful framework as we look more closely at the prayers of John Ames.

Adoration: Prayers of Hope to a Faithful God

Lord, you have been our dwelling place
in all generations.
Before the mountains were brought forth,
or ever you had formed the earth and the world,
from everlasting to everlasting you are God.
You turn us back to dust,
and say, "Turn back, you mortals."
For a thousand years in your sight
are like yesterday when it is past,
or like a watch in the night. (Ps. 90:1–4)

Dietrich Bonhoeffer called the book of Psalms the "Prayer Book of the Bible" in his book of the same title (*Psalms: The Prayer Book of the Bible,* Minneapolis: Augsburg, 1970). As we explore the various prayers of John Ames, it will be helpful to explore the Psalms as well. Psalm 90, for example, can be understood as a prayer of adoration, one that expresses a deep trust in God and an awe of the power and magnitude of God's being. This sense of awe is something like what Ames experienced as he anticipated his coming death. Just as the faithful prayers of the Psalms express adoration for a mighty and powerful God, Ames's expressions of faith can also be seen as prayers of adoration. Not all his musings took the form of a prayer addressed to God, but we hear in his words the confidence of a life lived in faith and his adoration for the God who gives him hope.

"The fact is, I don't want to be old. And I certainly don't want to be dead," Ames admitted (141). He loved his life—his family, his friends, his home—and already mourned the coming loss of it. This mourning, however, was balanced with a deep hope for the future, a hope supported by his faith in God's promises. Anyone who has moved from one beloved place to another where an exciting future awaits can perhaps relate to this feeling. Excitement about the new adventure is tempered by the sadness of leaving. "I've often been sorry to see a night end," Ames wrote, "even while I have loved seeing the dawn come" (71).

The dawn was coming for John Ames, the dawn that comes after death; he was quite aware of its nearness and inevitability. He had watched his good friend Boughton become frailer with age: "Now he's so bent over I don't know how you'd calculate his height...He says he's been reduced to a heap of joints, and not one of them works. You'd never know what he once was, looking at him now" (38). Ames no doubt saw something of himself in that image. He knew others around him were aware of his impending death as well: Lila and their son visited the cemetery where he would be buried; the ladies of his congregation, and of the Presbyterian congregation, were on standby ready to make casseroles at the drop of a hat.

Ames looked ahead to times when he would no longer be around and imagined what life in Gilead would be like without him. It was a hopeful sort of imagining. He expected good things to come to those he loved, and he was glad for that, if a bit sorry that he would not experience it himself. He knew, for example, that his congregation was thinking of building a new building and admitted that it was rather kind of them to wait until he was gone before tearing the old church down. He imagined that his family would move on. Lila was still young and might marry someone else; he even went so far as to consider Jack Boughton for that role.

Ames hoped many things for his young son, whose life sprawled out in front of him. He hoped he would grow up to be a faithful man; he hoped he would be well read. He expected that the boy would probably leave the town of Gilead and felt sadness in that. But he also experienced a hope that his son would find adventure in a good life elsewhere. "There are many ways to live a good life," he wrote (3). Ames's adoration of God manifested itself in trust. He entrusted the boy to God's care and offered a prayer that was whispered throughout the pages of this long letter and finally found voice in the closing words: "I'll pray that you grow up a brave man in a brave country. I will pray you find a way to be useful. I'll pray, and then I'll sleep" (247).

Ames was quite aware of the death that awaited him at that closing sleep. As a pastor in Gilead for so many years, he was no doubt witness to myriad deaths, some tragic, perhaps; some sudden; many natural and healthy and peaceful. Being present at these many deaths—such as that of Lacey Thrush, who wanted to say the Lord's Prayer and the Twenty-third Psalm, and "to hear 'When I Survey the Wondrous Cross' one last time" (57)—no doubt gave Ames much to think about as he anticipated his own death: "I have worried some about those last hours. This is another thing you know and I don't—how this ends. That is to say, how my life will seem to you to have ended" (73).

In these words we see an important facet of Ames's faith. His earthly life would soon be ended; to his son and wife, his life would be over. But Ames's Christian faith promised him a life beyond this life on earth, and this hereafter was something Ames spent much time thinking about and imagining. "This morning I have been trying to think about heaven, but without much success. I don't know why I should expect to have any idea of heaven. I could never have imagined this world if I hadn't spent almost eight decades walking around in it" (66).

But in fact, Ames did have some expectations of heaven. He imagined a place in which we are restored to all the fullness of our lives and reunited with all those we love who have gone before. He wrote to his son:

> While you read this, I am imperishable, somehow more alive than I have ever been, in the strength of my youth, with dear ones beside me. You read the dreams of an anxious, fuddled old man, and I live in a light better than any dream of mine—not waiting for you, though, because I want your dear perishable self to live long and to love this poor perishable world, which I somehow cannot imagine not missing bitterly, even while I do long to see what it will mean to have wife and child restored to me, I mean Louisa and Rebecca. I have wondered about that for many years. Well, this old seed is about to drop into the ground. Then I'll know. (*Gilead,* 53)

The hope of heaven even offered a hope for future reconciliation with Jack Boughton: "I will ask him how he [broke the window pane so that it shattered completely], someday when our souls are at peace and we can laugh about it" (182).

These prayers of hope express Ames's adoration of a God who makes such seemingly impossible reconciliations possible and who offers a glorious eternal life after death. An important distinction needs to be made here: Ames's prayers of hope were not of hope in the sense of wishing, as in "I hope it doesn't rain." Rather, he had hope in the sense of faith: He had hope—faith—in an eternal life after death. His belief in the goodness and faithfulness of God allowed him to face his death assured of a contented future for himself and for his family.

Confession: Prayers of Doubt and Regret

John Ames was, as we have seen, a man of deep faith and deep conviction. He was convinced of the goodness of life, the goodness of God, and the power of prayer. His life, however, was not without moments of doubt. It is normal and healthy for faithful believers to have times of uncertainty. The words of Psalm 22 betray a fear that God has ceased to be faithful: "My God, my God, why have you forsaken me? / Why are you so far from helping me, from the words of my groaning? / O my God, I cry by day, but you do not answer; / and by night, but find no rest" (Ps. 22:1–2). On the cross Jesus repeats the opening words of Psalm 22 (Mk. 15:34), offering up his final prayer to God.

One of Jesus' disciples, the famous "Doubting Thomas," refused to believe in Christ's resurrection until he had seen and touched Jesus' wounds (Jn. 20:24–25).

The way John Ames dealt with his doubts, the gaps in his knowledge about God and how God works, was to confess that he didn't and would never understand. The word *confession*, when used in this context, holds a double meaning: A *confession* of faith is an affirmative statement of belief, as in, "I confess that Jesus is the Christ, Son of the Living God." However, *confession* may also be used to describe an admission of sins: "I confess that I have sinned before God." We find both meanings of the word in Ames's prayers of confession. Sometimes, he confessed his inadequacies or his sins; at other times, he confessed his faith in God. Occasionally, his confession embodied both meanings: His admission that he did not understand God was also a statement of his faith in the great mystery of the Divine.

Faith is impossible to prove. Ames understood that "there are certain attributes our faith assigns to God: omniscience, omnipotence, justice, and grace. We human beings have such a slight acquaintance with power and knowledge, so little conception of justice, and so slight a capacity for grace, that the workings of these great attributes together is a mystery we cannot hope to penetrate" (150). For Ames, God was a mystery, and believing in that mystery was a part of believing in God. Becoming comfortable with the mystery of the unknown nature of God and confessing his inability to understand was a part of Ames's journey of faith.

Ames acknowledged that even the existence of God is a matter of unsolvable debate. A "problem in vocabulary" kept him from truly being able to explain or understand the existence of God. He advised his son:

> So my advice is this—don't look for proofs. Don't bother with them at all. They are never sufficient to the question, and they're always a little impertinent, I think, because they claim for God a place within our conceptual grasp…

> I'm not saying never doubt or question. The Lord gave you a mind so that you would make honest use of it. (*Gilead,* 179)

The conversation Ames had with Boughton, Jack, and Lila about predestination (a conversation Glory chose to leave, claiming to have heard all the arguments many times before) provides a good example. Jack was looking for straightforward answers, but Ames knew there was no such thing:

> "That's a complicated issue."
>
> "Let me simplify it," [Jack] said. "Do you think some people are intentionally and irretrievably consigned to perdition?"
>
> "Well," I said, "That may actually be the kind of simplification that raises more questions than it avoids." (*Gilead,* 150)

Ames was not one to be content with simple answers to tough questions. He wrestled with the deep quandaries of faith, confessed his doubts, and was confident enough in his God and in his faith to be comfortable with an unsolvable problem. As dear Boughton put it, "To conclude is not in the nature of the enterprise" (152).

Ames's willingness to question and doubt helped him as he wrestled with his life's greatest challenges. His most powerful confession was that he did not know how to deal with Jack Boughton: He believed that he was called to forgive and reconcile with his godson, but he couldn't fathom how to do so. Jack's ill-fated involvement with the younger girl challenged his greatest convictions: "Where wisdom could have found a place in a situation like that one I don't claim to know" (157), and later: "I don't know the right and wrong of a situation like that" (159). But his faith did lead him to spend much time in prayer over Jack Boughton. In the end, his confession of inadequacy and his willingness to struggle helped him to see that grace is, after all, sufficient.

Thanksgiving: Prayers of a Joy-filled Life

The Psalms are full of expressions of thanksgiving. Psalm 100, for example, concludes: "Enter his gates with thanksgiving, / and his courts with praise. / Give thanks to him, bless his name. / For the Lord is good; / his steadfast love endures forever, / and his faithfulness to all generations" (Ps. 100:4–5). Ames lived his life in the spirit of this psalm, giving thanks to God for all the goodness in the world, even giving thanks for existence itself. Ames had great appreciation for the subtle details of life. It was not grand celebrations or momentous events that brought him joy; it was having breakfast with his wife and child, the way the sunlight played on the carpeted floor, the way Soapy the cat perched on his son's back as he drew pictures of airplanes. Robinson's gentle descriptions of such precious moments show us that they are, in fact, part of Ames's prayer of thanksgiving.

On the morning of Ames's seventy-seventh birthday, great joy reigned in the Ames household. Lila served pancakes and "nice little sausages," and the table was adorned with flowers. Ames's son had learned the Beatitudes, and proudly recited them, twice, for his father. Despite the constant reminder that his heart was in its last days—or perhaps because of it—Ames dearly appreciated this tender celebration: "I hate to think what I would give for a thousand mornings like this. For two or three. You were wearing your red shirt and your mother was wearing her blue dress" (185).

Ames found his deepest joy in the love of his wife, Lila. It is not insignificant that she wandered into his life, into his church, "in the middle of the prayer" (19). Lila was the source of contentment and fulfillment after many years of grief, loneliness, and emptiness. For Ames, loving her was akin to loving God:

> I might seem to be comparing something great and holy with a minor and ordinary thing, that is, love of God with mortal love. But I just don't see them as separate things at all. If we can be divinely fed with a morsel and divinely blessed with a touch, then the terrible pleasure we find in a particular face can certainly instruct us in the nature of the very grandest love. I devoutly believe this to be true. (*Gilead*, 204)

Ames looked at his son with similar awe and pleasure. The boy had been "God's grace" to him, bringing him such joy, allowing him to experience fatherhood at such a late age. Ames treasured moments with his son: the boy sitting on his lap as he drew pictures, drinking honeysuckle from wildflowers, waiting on the porch in anticipation of sandwiches of peanut butter and apple butter on raisin bread. "Children seem to think every pleasant thing has to be a surprise" (117).

Because he was childless for so long and because he knew their time together would be short, Ames viewed his son with a sense of amazement that he would never take for granted. He noticed the light on his hair, the color of his skin. "I suppose you're not prettier than most children," he wrote. "You're just a nice-looking boy, a bit slight, well scrubbed and well mannered. All that is fine, but it's your existence I love you for, mainly. Existence seems to me now the most remarkable thing that could ever be imagined" (52–53).

In fact, Ames spent a great deal of time thinking about—and giving thanks for—existence. The preciousness of life, even the sorrows of life, were made all the more amazing by the very fact of life itself. He believed that existence is relational: "[A] thing that does not exist in relation to anything else cannot itself be said to exist" (47). His relationships with his family and friends, then, took on all the more importance; relationships are what make life what it is. As we discussed in the previous chapter, Ames was deeply influenced by Feuerbach's *The Essence of Christianity*. He especially remembered this passage: "'Only that which is apart from my own being is capable of being doubted by me. How then can I doubt of God, who is my being? To doubt of God is to doubt of myself'" (239). Ames took this to heart: his expressions of gratefulness for the life he lived were no less than a song of thanksgiving to the God whose very being makes life possible.

Supplication: Prayers for Comfort in Hard Times

Prayers of supplication are appeals to God, often asking for something for ourselves or on behalf of someone else. These sorts of prayers are often used in times of difficulty or sorrow. Consider this prayer, from Psalm 88: "O LORD, God of my salvation, / when, at night, I cry out in your presence, / let my prayer come before you; / incline your ear to my cry. / For my soul is full of troubles, / and my life draws near to Sheol" (Ps. 88:1–3).

For John Ames, prayer was a source of comfort through many of life's troubles. He understood that sorrow is a part of all human life, and dealing with it is part of the life of faith: "I heard a man say once that Christians worship sorrow. That is by no means true. But we do believe there is a sacred mystery in it, it's fair to say that" (137). Certainly a great deal of sorrow had filled John Ames's life, not just personal sadness, though there was plenty of that as well, but also sorrow in the life of the community he served. Illness, war, and poverty touched the town of Gilead throughout the years. The sorrow and tragedy of the Civil War lingered on in his memory, even though it was not in his lifetime. He shared the sorrow and anguish of the Boughton family at the disappointment Jack caused. Through all these hard times, he turned to prayer for comfort, grace, and peace.

It is an interesting commentary on the nature of prayer that Ames did not, usually, pray *for* something in particular; rather, he often prayed "over" concerns or troubles. On dark nights when he couldn't sleep, he walked through town praying that those people in the houses he walked by might have peace—not that their problems be solved or erased, but that they come to some reconciliation with their situation. As he sat in his church, watching the sunrise bring light into the room, he felt a calm, even in the midst of trouble: "I felt much at peace those mornings, praying over very dreadful things sometimes—the Depression, the wars. That was a lot of misery for people around here, decades of it. But prayer brings peace, as I trust you know" (70).

Even his prayers about Jack Boughton eventually brought peace, though this seems to be the most troublesome of the sorrows Ames addressed. He had been praying about Jack Boughton for all his life, it seemed—at least since his baptism as "John Ames Boughton" made the boy a constant reminder of his own childlessness. When Jack got himself in trouble, Ames turned to prayer with his old friend Boughton, a testament both to their deep friendship and their commitment to and confidence in prayer. Ames remembered:

> Not so many years ago I was sitting at that table in the dark eating cold meat loaf from the pan it came in, listening to the radio, when old Boughton let himself in the door and sat down at the table and said, "Don't put the light on." So I turned the radio off and we sat there together and talked and prayed, about John Ames Boughton, for John Ames Boughton. (*Gilead,* 121)

The trouble Jack got into and the grief he caused his family brought great discomfort for Ames, so much so that he found it difficult, if not impossible, to forgive Jack. Despite his deep faith and conviction that God's grace is wide enough for all manner of sin, he did not know how to reconcile this relationship. Ames knew that his inability to forgive Jack was a failing on his part, and prayed about that as well. When Jack paid an unexpected visit one afternoon, Ames left "to look over some things at the church…I spent several hours in meditation and prayer over John Ames Boughton, and also over John Ames, the father of his soul" (123).

As in other times of distress, Ames did not pray for a particular outcome, rather, he prayed for guidance and wisdom to handle the situation well. Even in this difficult circumstance, his prayers brought him comfort: "I believe I am beginning to see where the grace is for me in this. I have prayed considerably, and I have slept awhile, too, and I feel I am reaching some clarity" (201).

Prayer and Practice

What is *prayer,* actually? It seems to take on so many forms and to be defined in so many ways that it is often hard to pin down what exactly we are doing when we pray. It's a slippery term, incorporating everything from "please" and "thank you," to "why?" and "why not?" For John Ames, prayer was sometimes spoken, sometimes written, sometimes silent. Prayer is sometimes full of curiosity, sometimes full of conviction, often full of hope, or fear, or pleading. The *Merriam Webster Dictionary* defines prayer as "a supplication or expression addressed to God or a god…" The *Oxford English Dictionary* is more specific: "a request for help or expression of thanks addressed to God or another deity."

These definitions emphasize "addressing" God, and that certainly describes many prayers. But such definitions also imply a formality and a use of words that are not always necessary for prayer. Must prayer always be in the form of words, spoken or silent? Could prayer also be simply sitting in the presence of God? Does prayer always involve "addressing," or is prayer sometimes listening? The *Harper-Collins Dictionary of Catholicism* offers this definition: "Prayer is the act by which one enters into conscious, loving communion with God." You might consider how you would define prayer.

As difficult as it is to define prayer, it is even harder to describe how prayer works. We sometimes imagine prayer to be a simple format: We ask for something—rain for our crops—and God provides. But it is rarely as straightforward as that. The question of how God answers prayer is answered differently by anyone who has ever prayed. Was Lila's entrance into John Ames's church "in the middle of the prayer" an answer to his decades of lonely prayers? Kathleen Norris, a writer and theologian, addresses this question by writing, "I have learned that prayer is not asking for what you think you want but asking to be changed in ways you can't imagine…People who are in the habit of praying…know that when a prayer is answered, it is never in a way that you expect" (*Amazing Grace,* New York: Riverhead Books. 1998, 61).

Prayer in the Bible

The Bible, even, does not give us a singular definition of prayer. Instead, we see throughout the Hebrew and Christian scriptures a variety of styles, forms, and circumstances for prayer. In the early chapters of Genesis, Adam interacted with an anthropomorphic God who walked about in the garden and spoke to him. Likewise, Abraham spoke directly with God, responding to what God called him to do. Later, when the Israelites were enslaved in Egypt, they raised their prayers to God, who heard their cries and saved them. The prayers of Job, lifted up to God in the midst of tragedy around him, portrayed his deep faith. The prayers of kings, prophets, and other leaders often came in the form of visions or dreams.

We have already seen that the Psalms provide examples of many types of prayers, and are perhaps the richest source of prayers in the Bible. The Psalter can be understood as an ancient hymnbook; the Psalms were originally composed for use in public worship settings. Many of the Psalms are songs of praise, others are cries of lament, still others are expressions of faith and trust or retellings of Israel's history. Many other examples of prayers lifted to God appear throughout the Hebrew Scriptures. You might find it helpful to page through the Psalms, or another Old Testament book, and look for the different forms prayers take.

Likewise, prayer in the Christian Testament is neither uniform nor well-defined. In the gospels, Jesus most notably offered prayers at critical junctures in his ministry: his baptism, the calling of his disciples, his transfiguration, and his crucifixion. In the garden of Gethsemane just before he was arrested, Jesus prayed, "My Father, if it is possible, let this cup pass from me; yet not what I want but what you want" (Mt. 26:39). Here we see Jesus in supplication while still yielding himself to God's will. Jesus' prayers from the cross give us further insight into Jesus' prayer life.

Jesus did give some guidance on prayer. He warned against showy prayers, and against praying so that others would see and be impressed. Instead, he said, "But whenever you pray, go into your room and shut the door and pray to your Father who is in secret" (Mt. 6:6). Jesus also presented an image of a God who hears and answers prayers: "Ask, and it will be given you; search, and you will find; knock, and the door will be opened for you. For everyone who asks receives, and everyone who searches finds, and for everyone who knocks, the door will be opened" (Mt. 7:7–8). Jesus presented the Lord's Prayer (Mt. 6:9–13), perhaps the most famous of Christian prayers, as a way for his followers to pray.

The New Testament letters also provide a model of prayer. Similar to the letter of John Ames, the letters of Paul can be considered prayers in and of themselves. Paul gave thanks for those to whom he was writing, lifted up their concerns and struggles, and prayed for continued strength and blessings. Paul, along with the other New Testament letter writers, prayed for accord within the new movement, growth of the church, and a strengthening of the faith of its members. This prayer, from Romans 15:5–6, is a good example:

> May the God of steadfastness and encouragement grant you to live in harmony with one another, in accordance with Christ Jesus, so that together you may with one voice glorify the God and Father of our Lord Jesus Christ.

Practicing Prayer

What do we learn from the prayers of John Ames? Perhaps we learn to give thanks even for the small joys of life. We learn to pray through hardship, grief, and doubt. We learn to pray for hope. From Ames, we learn to pray for wisdom, guidance, and peace for ourselves and for those we love.

When we look at *how* Ames prayed, we gain even more wisdom. Ames set aside certain times for praying: Like many ministers, he took Mondays off for prayer and rest. He also had special places that were, for him, places for prayer—the church before dawn, for example. You might consider where the times and places for prayer are in your own life. Ames also, however, showed us that any time and any place is the right time for prayer: in his armchair in the living room, on the dusty roads of Kansas, at the kitchen table with an old friend.

Despite all we can learn from observing the prayers of John Ames, however, we might consider other ways that we in the twenty-first century can learn to pray. Prayer has always been intended to be both private and public, personal and communal. Prayers are offered in the quiet of our own homes as well as with a congregation of worshipers. In the end, the ways in which we bring ourselves into the presence of the Divine have no limit.

We come before God sometimes to listen, sometimes to speak, sometimes to sing, sometimes to dance. Maybe you pray by setting aside time each morning when you light a candle and spend a few moments in silence. Maybe you pray by participating in morning or evening prayer services at a local church; maybe you follow the ancient tradition of praying the hours by stopping to pray at fixed times during the day. Some people pray by reading and studying. Some pray through meditation, or by journaling. Some people find that using a tangible object such as a rosary or prayer beads helps them to pray; others find prayer partners to encourage and support them on their journey. No experiences are too big or too small to be appropriate for prayer; prayer is not an art to be perfected, but a practice to be lived.

QUESTIONS FOR DISCUSSION

1. We discussed four types of prayers: adoration, confession, thanksgiving, and supplication. Are there other types? Can you find other examples of these prayers in *Gilead* or in the Bible?
2. What role does prayer play in your life? What forms of prayer are most effective for you?
3. How does God answer prayers? How do we know when a prayer has been answered?
4. How do you imagine "heaven"? What do you believe about life after death? In what ways is heaven in your prayers?
5. How did prayer help John Ames work through difficult situations? How did prayer bring him peace?

For Further Reading

Dietrich Bonhoeffer, *Psalms: The Prayer Book of the Bible*. Minneapolis: Augsburg , 1970.

Joseph D. Driskill, *Protestant Spiritual Exercises: Theology, History, and Practice*. Harrisburg, Pa.: Morehouse, 1999.

Kathleen Norris, *Amazing Grace: A Vocabulary of Faith*. New York: Riverhead Books, 1998.

Kay Bessler Northcutt, *Praying By Heart: Prayers for Personal Devotion and Public Worship*. Cleveland: United Church Press, 1998.

J. Bradley Wigger, *Together We Pray: A Prayer Book for Families*. St. Louis: Chalice Press, 2005.

CHAPTER 4

Remembering Life

Remember the days of old,
consider the years long past;
ask your father, and he will inform you;
your elders, and they will tell you.

(Deut. 32:7)

My father was born in Kansas, as I was, because the old man had come there from Maine just to help Free Soilers establish the right to vote, because the constitution was going to be voted on that would decide whether Kansas entered the Union slave or free. Quite a few people went out there at that time for that reason. And, of course, so did people from Missouri who wanted Kansas for the South. So things were badly out of hand for awhile. All best forgotten, my father used to say. He didn't like mention of those times, and that did cause some hard feelings between him and his father. I've read up on those events considerably, and I've decided my father was right. And that's just as well, because people have forgotten. Remarkable things went on, certainly, but there has been so much trouble in the world since then it's hard to find time to think about Kansas.

(Gilead, 75–76)

The game of baseball hasn't changed all that much in the two hundred years it has been in existence. Technological advances, Little League fathers, drug scandals, and labor disputes have affected the game in small ways, but three strikes are still an out, six outs are still an inning. Kids still play in alleyways after school; a hot dog in the stands on a sunny summer day still beats spending the afternoon in the office.

Every generation in the Ames family appreciated baseball. Ames I took his grandson to see Bud Fowler play in Des Moines in the 1890s, and Edward played catch with his little brother when he returned from Germany. In the 1950s, Jack Boughton taught the youngest Ames how to catch and throw while the dying Ames III watched the Yankees and Red Sox on his new television set.

Some things don't change much with time; others do. In this chapter, we'll focus on remembering life, not just the life of John Ames, but the history of the entire Ames family. In doing so, we'll raise the question Ames himself raised: Is it better to remember or forget? Did remembering the conflict between his father and grandfather help him move beyond it, or did it merely drag up old wounds? Did telling the story of Jack's illegitimate child help him come to terms with the situation, or did it keep him from forgiving his godson?

We'll start out by looking at the historical context of this novel, which is important to its themes. Then we'll turn to the relationships between the fathers and sons in *Gilead* and explore the relationship patterns that all generations go through. Finally, we'll take a look back at important journeys and significant legacies of the Ames family. Perhaps we will find that looking back to the past is an important step in the process of looking ahead to the future.

Bleeding Kansas

The historical backdrop of *Gilead* is vital to the story, and Robinson assumes a certain level of knowledge of Kansas history. If it has been more than a few years since you studied American history in high school, you may find a refresher helpful.

With the acquisition of the Louisiana Purchase in 1803, the new United States of America doubled in size, and cries of "Manifest Destiny!" convinced people to move westward to the new territories. As the country grew, so did one of its most troublesome questions: Should new states admitted to the union allow slavery? Plantation owners in the south, who had a financial interest in the question, answered yes; northern abolitionists opposed to slavery said no. In the 1850's, Kansas got caught in the middle.

Ames III says that his grandfather came to Kansas from Maine as a Free Soiler in the 1830s. He would not have been alone. For years, people from New England moved westward. Some went in search of adventure or more land, some in support of ideological causes such as the abolition of slavery. In fact, organizations like the New England Emigrant Aid Society were formed for the sole purpose of encouraging and enabling settlers to move west and claim Kansas as a free state. Religious leaders also organized convoys west, and settlers were soon sporting "Beecher's Bibles," which were actually Sharps rifles supplied for the cause by New York's Rev. Henry Ward Beecher.

Politics, of course, played a significant role in the shaping of Kansas history. Three acts of Congress in the decades before the Civil War are important to understand:

Missouri Compromise: In 1820, Missouri was admitted as a slave state, along with the free state of Maine. The compromise stated that this pattern of one slave and one free state would continue as later states were admitted. More importantly, however, the compromise held that slavery would be prohibited in the rest of the territories carved out of the Louisiana Purchase, an area that included Kansas.

Compromise of 1850: This act admitted California as a free state and divided the rest of the land acquired from Mexico into the territories of Utah and New Mexico, which later would be admitted to the union as free or slave states, according to the wishes of the settlers there. Included in this compromise, and what made it so significant, was a stronger fugitive slave act that denied runaway slaves the right to a trial by jury. This angered northern abolitionists and strengthened their resolve to help escaped slaves to freedom.

Kansas-Nebraska Act: In 1854, this act repealed the Missouri Compromise by stating that the territories of the Louisiana Purchase could decide for themselves whether to be free or slave states. Free Soilers, who had believed Kansas would become a free state based on the earlier Missouri Compromise, now found themselves fighting pro-slavery factions for control of the state.

This led to a period of violence along the Missouri-Kansas border, which came to be known as "Bleeding Kansas." Pro-slavery advocates from Missouri crossed into Kansas and clashed with abolitionists from the north. Anti-slavery "Jayhawkers" assaulted slave owners, freed slaves, looted property, then helped the escaped slaves move north along the Underground Railroad.

Such was the setting for a number of important episodes in *Gilead.* In the story of the horse that fell through the road, the town was building a tunnel precisely for the purpose of hiding escaped slaves. Ames remembered that Gilead was a stop on the Underground Railroad: "Several houses in town have hidden cellars or cabinets where people could be put out of sight for a day or two. The church has one in the attic" (158). Ames also mentioned that his grandfather was friends with Jim Lane and John Brown, two important anti-slavery figures in the Bleeding Kansas era.

Jim Lane: Known for his zealous orations, Jim Lane was a politician who came to Kansas in the early 1850s and quickly became a leader in the free-state movement. He helped organize the Topeka Constitution in an attempt to have Kansas admitted to the union as a free state. He was effective in rallying people to the cause and helped organize abolitionists from as far away as Chicago to fight against the pro-slavery forces.

John Brown: Osawatomie John Brown, as he was called, or "Old Brown"—a nickname he acquired for living into his fifties when most men in the area were in their twenties or thirties—was something of a legend in his own time. He was tall and fiery, and it is said that insanity ran in his family; he was an angry and violent man, impassioned by the cause of abolitionism. A leader in the Kansas militia in the mid-1850s, he called for the free-state movement to respond with force to the pro-slavery violence.

The conflict reached a head in May 1956, when a pro-slavery police force raided Lawrence, Kansas, an abolitionist stronghold. The newspaper offices of the *Herald of Freedom* and the *Kansas Free State* were destroyed, and other free-state leaders' homes were looted and burned. In retaliation, Brown and his sons led a raid on Pottawatomie Creek, brutally killing and mutilating five pro-slavery settlers. Free-staters hailed the massacre as a victory, but the violence only escalated into a guerilla war along the Missouri-Kansas border that lasted throughout the summer of 1856.

Brown is most famous for leading a raid on a federal arsenal in Harper's Ferry, Virginia, in 1859. With a number of other men, including several of his sons, he planned to steal weapons from the arsenal, free the slaves in the area, and arm them to join in the fight. The raid failed, however. Brown was wounded and captured, convicted of treason, and executed shortly afterwards.

When the young Ames II woke in the night to find men and horses in the church, he learned that his father (Ames I) was involved with John Brown and had gone to help a freed slave escape. That night, Ames II discovered a violent streak in his father, a discovery that opened a gulf between the father and son that would continue to widen throughout and beyond the Civil War. Sadly, the gulf would never completely close.

Fathers and Sons

The story of the Ames family spans four generations, from Ames I's move from Maine to Kansas in the 1830s to Ames III's seventy-seventh birthday with his son in the 1950s. The way Robinson has written *Gilead* makes the family tree almost circular rather than linear. Relationships between the Ames fathers and sons intertwine throughout the novel, with each generation echoing or foreshadowing another. To help us explore some of the significant father/son relationships in *Gilead,* we return to the motif of the prodigal son, which we first discussed in chapter 2. In the gospel parable (Lk. 15:11–32), the son rebels against his father and his tradition by squandering his inheritance, then comes to regret his choices, and finally returns home and reconciles with his family. This pattern of rebellion, regret, and reconciliation manifests itself from generation to generation in the *Gilead* relationships. Each generation needs its own rebellion and its own return home.

Rebellion

We first encounter rebellion in *Gilead* through the relationship between Ames III's older brother Edward and their father. Edward was expected to become a great preacher, like his father and grandfather before him, but when he came home from studying in Europe, his family found that he had changed significantly. He could quote scripture accurately and had a thorough knowledge of theology, but could no longer, "in good conscience," say grace before dinner (26). His time away made him reexamine his belief system; much to his father's shame and disappointment, he declared himself an atheist and left the vocation of ministry to his younger brother, John.

Jack Boughton's rebellion began when he was young, with routine juvenile delinquent behavior, vandalism, and petty theft. Gradually it grew into trouble with the law, culminating in the relationship with the girl that led to the illegitimate child. Jack's ultimate rebellion was his refusal to take responsibility for his actions, or even to acknowledge the child he had fathered. He fled Gilead, leaving his parents and sister to deal with the situation. In Ames's view, Jack had completely rejected his father's values.

The relationship between Ames I and Ames II is one of the most complex in the novel. From early on, they had different outlooks on life. Ames I valued freedom over all else, and that end would justify any means he used to achieve it, including violence. In his Fourth of July speech just before leaving for his final trip to Kansas, he declared, echoing Luke 4:18, that his calling was to "Free the captive. Preach good news to the poor. Proclaim liberty throughout the land" (175). Ames II, on the other hand, valued peace above all else. In an argument with his father he said, "My hopes are in peace, and I am not disappointed. Because peace is its own reward. Peace is its own justification" (84).

As a young boy, Ames II first recognized this difference between himself and his father. This occurred on the night when Ames I helped a slave escape and encountered an enemy soldier along the way. Ames II's loyalty to his father was still strong, however; he continued to clean up the mess in the church and was relieved when no one came looking for the missing soldier. Later in his life, the conflict between father and son became more pronounced. After the Civil War, Ames II went to "sit with the Quakers on the Sabbath," while his father preached to his own dying congregation about the "divine righteousness manifested" in the destruction of the war (87). (Quakers are a religious group dedicated to pacifism; many Quakers were active abolitionists and assisted on the Underground Railroad.)

Ames II shouted to his father, "I remember when you walked to the pulpit in that shot-up, bloody shirt with that pistol in your belt. And I had a thought as powerful and clear as any revelation. And it was, This has *nothing* to do with Jesus. Nothing. Nothing" (84–5). These two men who were alike in many ways, especially in their passion for their vocation, held fundamentally different views about how to live out their faith, and this fundamental difference was the root of rebellion.

Even Ames III rebelled in a small way against his father. Interestingly, his rebellion had to do with staying where he was rather than going somewhere else, as was the case in the other father/son relationships. After moving to the Gulf Coast, Ames II tried to convince Ames III to also move away from Gilead, saying that he need not be loyal to the "very old and even very local" ideas the family had instilled in him (235). Ames III, however, took offense; they were *his* values and principles now, as well. Ames III's rebellion was not as dramatic as his older brother's, but it was a claim of independence all the same.

Claiming independence is essentially what such rebellions are about. For all children, growing up also means growing away, finding their own identity apart from their parents. Notice that even the older son in Luke's parable rebels against his father, who welcomes the prodigal home. Sometimes, children have to push hard to get far enough away to find out who they are. Part of a healthy coming-of-age requires some letting go of former identities and values. The line between healthy rebellion and destructive behavior is sometimes a thin one, however, as any parent of teenagers knows. The teen who rebels so much that he is harmful to himself or others (Jack Boughton is a good example) has gone past the point of healthy rebellion. On the other extreme is the child who never rebels and never learns to truly see herself as a person apart from her family of origin.

Interestingly, many of the fathers in *Gilead* also rebelled in some way against their sons. Ames III is the best example, in his unintended rejection of Jack. We also might see him as rebelling against his younger son, again unintentionally, by dying before he was able to share his life with him. Ames II rebelled against his younger son by moving to Florida, leaving the newly widowed Ames III with a pulpit and a broken-down church building. Do you think that father-rebellion is as much a part of the father/son relationship as rebellion on the part of the son?

Regret

In Luke's parable, the son regretted his decision to leave home the moment he found himself eating dinner with the swine. In each of the father/son relationships in *Gilead*, rebellion was followed by deep regret by at least one party in the relationship. Regret comes in different forms: Sometimes the fathers or sons regret specific actions; at other times, they simply regret that the relationship has ruptured in some way. We aren't privy to Edward's side of the story, but Ames II was clearly upset by his older son's rejection of his faith and his way of life, so much so, in fact, that he deviated from his normal practice and referred to the situation from the pulpit. Likewise, Ames III mentioned that he and his father had often disappointed one another, and he regretted that fact.

Ames II felt a great deal of regret surrounding his relationship with his father. He regretted worshiping with the Quakers after the Civil War, especially when he saw how it affected his mother. His frustration at their differences in opinion continued until Ames I finally left for Kansas. Even then, he regretted how they parted. Ames III wrote, "It grieved my father bitterly that the last words he said to his father were very angry words and there could never be any reconciliation between them in this life. He did truly honor his father, generally speaking, and it was hard for him to accept that things should have ended the way they did" (10).

Even Jack Boughton came to regret the strain in his relationship with his father and with Ames III. Though he didn't offer any apology for his behavior or articulate any regret for the life of his illegitimate child, he showed his regret in other ways. When talking to Ames III about following Ames II into the ministry, Jack said, "It's an enviable thing, to be able to receive your identity from your father" (168). Was this an acknowledgement that he had not lived up to his own father's expectations of him?

Regret appears to be a post-rebellion necessity for sons and a requirement for fathers. Just by having children, parents seem destined to at least some level of guilt and regret about how they cared for or related to their children. In just seven years, Ames III developed regrets over his young son. He regretted dying so soon and leaving him fatherless, and he regretted spending all his money on books before he was married so that there was nothing left to leave his son. Regret, it seems, is part of the equation of growing up and moving on. Without rebellion, we don't achieve independence; without regret, we cannot reconcile.

Reconciliation

The prodigal in Luke's story returned home to find his father waiting with open arms, ready to celebrate his return. Reunion is not always so simple in *Gilead,* but each of the father/son relationships does come to some sort of reconciliation. In some situations, the reconciliation is an unspoken truce, an agreement to put the past aside. This is apparently the case with Edward and Ames II, who reconciled at least enough to spend their retirements on the Gulf Coast together. In the same way, the Boughton family seemed to find some reconciliation with Jack, so that Glory and the older Boughton enjoyed having him at home.

Ames II was not able to reconcile with his father until after the latter's death. The journey to Kansas to find Ames I's grave provided the closure Ames II needed for this relationship. Once he found the grave, he and Ames III spent all day cleaning the small graveyard, planting seeds, and "putting things to rights" (13). He could no longer care for his father, so caring for his grave would have to suffice. He knelt in prayer for a long time at the grave, before looking up to see the brilliant light between the sun and the moon. Before leaving the graveyard, he gave voice to the reconciliation that had taken place: "I would never have thought this place could be beautiful. I'm glad to know that" (15).

The most difficult reconciliation in *Gilead* is that between Jack Boughton and Ames III. The relationship was complex for many reasons, and it was not always clear what needed to be reconciled between the two of them. Ames constantly found himself drawing back from Jack. He admitted that he felt some guilt toward Jack for the bitterness he felt at his baptism—having not been warned that the boy was to be named after him. Still grieving the loss of his own child, he understandably thought, "This is *not* my child," and later says that he had "never been able to warm to him, never" (188). He immediately recanted this statement, but it is clearly true that a distance separated Ames and his godson, a distance that felt too wide to cross. Ames felt the need to forgive Jack, but he also felt that it might not be his place to do so. Such thoughts further clouded the possibility for reconciliation:

> It is not for me to forgive Jack Boughton. Any harm he did to me personally was indirect, and really very minor...That one man should lose his child and the next man should just squander his fatherhood as if it were nothing—well, that does not mean that the second man has transgressed against the first. I don't forgive him. I wouldn't know where to begin. (*Gilead*, 164)

Likewise, Jack was uncomfortable around Ames, especially when he came to talk with him in the church, but neither of them was able to pinpoint what the offense had been. To complicate matters further, the Boughton family loved Jack fiercely; and they seemed to have forgiven—or at least forgotten—Jack's transgressions in a way that Ames could not. Nevertheless, the two sought reconciliation, with each other and with their present situations. When Jack came to see him at the church for the first time, his first words are "I'm very sorry." Jack was talking about waking him, but weren't those the very words Ames wanted to hear from him? It is worth considering how Ames came to peace with his relationship with Jack. In the end, Ames found reconciliation by following his own advice: "remembering and forgiving can be contrary things" (164). After learning about Jack's wife and child, he was ready to look forward instead of back, celebrating Jack's new family instead of remembering old transgressions; and in doing so, he began to forgive.

As the relationship between Ames and Jack illustrates, reconciliation is rarely clean and tidy. In some ways, the gospel parable of the prodigal son gives us an idealized version of the father/son relationship pattern, with examples that are hard to live up to. It didn't take long for the son to swallow his pride, admit he was wrong, and return home with an apology. The father quickly welcomed him home, forgave his transgressions, and threw a party. Neither Jack nor Ames seemed capable of such behavior. The reconciliation they worked out was a more tenuous one.

It is also worth considering what all these father/son relationship patterns have to do with Ames's young son. The vast age difference between Ames and his son dramatically changed the dynamic between them. Ames would not live long enough to see his son's choices in life, to know what his rebellion would be. Even the minor transgressions Ames saw in his son—drawing fighter planes, playing with toy weapons—he refused to forbid; the son was not even aware that he was offending his father. Will the early death of Ames mean that his son will escape the rebellion/regret/return pattern? Or will the son still find something about his father, even if deceased, against which to rebel?

Bridging Past and Future

As one generation gives way to the next, some things help make the connection between the past and the future. Two of these connectors are journeys and legacies, both of which are important themes in *Gilead.* We often set out on journeys to look for our past, or to leave our past behind. We leave legacies, intangible legacies like family stories, or tangible ones like a waterlogged Greek Testament, so that our future will know our past. Journeys are the bridge from past to future; we always come home changed. Legacies are the things we turn to when we want to remember the past to look forward to the future.

Journeys

At one point or another all the major characters in *Gilead* went on a journey that had a significant impact on their lives. Some journeys were in search of the past. Some, such as Edward's journey to Europe, were in search of the future. All were catalysts of change. Edward returned from Germany physically changed—he sported a new mustache and a walking stick—as well as spiritually changed, claiming to be an atheist and rejecting the faith in which he had been raised. Edward's journey did, then, lead to a rejection of his past, but it pointed him toward his future as a college professor, which he carried out contentedly for many years.

The notion of a journey that connects our past to our future is prevalent in the Bible, as well. When God first spoke to Abram, he instructed him to take a journey: "Go from your country and your kindred and your father's house to the land that I will show you" (Gen. 12:1). Abram's life as the son of Terah was over; his life as Abraham, father of a nation, began with that journey. His descendant Joseph, sold into slavery, made the journey to Egypt and sealed the fate of generations of Hebrew people. Later, the exodus from Egypt became a significant journey in the history of Israel; for forty years, the people wandered in the desert before coming into the promised land. That journey served as a transition from their history as slaves to their future as a nation.

Shortly after his baptism, Jesus took a similar journey to the desert. On that journey, he was tempted by the devil and passed every test, returning to Galilee "filled with the power of the Spirit" and ready to begin his ministry (Lk. 4:14). In fact, all of Jesus' public ministry was a sort of journey, one that led him to Jerusalem and eventually to the cross. This trek to the cross, too, is a journey, one that reminds us that the past is over and the future is coming.

Ames I traveled on a number of journeys that marked significant changes in his life. Early in his life, he traveled from Maine to Kansas to start his new life there. After the Civil War, when his church dwindled and eventually died, he moved with his family to Gilead. The most important journey of his life, however, was his final trip to Kansas, a journey in search of the past rather than the future. He returned to what surely felt like home, to the scene of his glory days.

His death in Kansas prompted another important journey, that of Ames II and Ames III in search of his grave. As we have discussed, this journey was significant for many reasons. The trip was the occasion for bonding between father and son; Ames III heard many of the important family stories for the first time on those dusty roads. Like the period of the Israelites' wandering in the desert, the trip was a time of hardship for Ames III, such that he had not known before and hadn't since. "That journey was a great blessing to me," he remembered (17). Finding Ames I's grave was a journey that brought closure to his family. When Ames II and Ames III left the graveyard and headed back to Iowa, they were leaving one generation behind and looking ahead to the future.

Jack Boughton had at least two important journeys in *Gilead.* When his son was born in Memphis, he traveled there from St. Louis to find his wife and child. This was a significant journey because it contrasted so sharply with a journey Jack did *not* take earlier in his life; he took responsibility for this child in a way that he did not care for the first child he fathered. Although it hardly made up for damage already done, this journey did mark a significant change in Jack's life.

Jack's return to Gilead was another important journey, though its significance was complex. At first, it was not entirely clear why Jack had come home. Was it to see his dying father? to atone for past sins? to make peace with his family and his past? We discover, eventually, that he came in hopes of finding a way to bring Della and the child to live in Gilead. He told Ames, "I have even thought it might be a pleasure to introduce Robert to my father. I would like him to know that I finally have something I can be proud of" (229). He wanted to be a responsible husband and father and struggled to find a way to do so. In a way, Jack journeyed to his past in search of hope for the future.

Consider the important journeys you have taken in your life. Maybe it was a wrong turn off the highway that made you late for your meeting but led to a quiet back road you didn't know was there. Perhaps you took a long road trip with friends just after graduating from college, discovering new parts of the country and new parts of yourself. Or maybe you made a long, unexpected journey to be with a dying loved one, a journey that led to the healing of old hurts and quiet conversations with family in hospital waiting rooms. Wherever our journey leads us, whatever the circumstances, we no doubt come back with a new view of life.

Legacies

We have talked about intangible legacies, such as the stories passed down from generation to generation. We turn now to the tangible things, the physical legacies we leave behind when we leave this earth. Perhaps you have a piece of jewelry that has been passed down in your family for generations. Or maybe you have love letters written from your grandfather to your grandmother while he was overseas during a war. Maybe the rose bushes behind your house were planted by someone in your family generations ago and now bloom every spring in remembrance of days gone by. The sum of the legacies we leave do not add up to the whole of our lives, but they are tangible reminders of the life we lived.

The Bible provides us with examples of legacies passed down from generation to generation. Scripture itself is one such legacy. First passed down orally, then written on scrolls and later in books, the ancient scriptures serve as reminders of the faith of the ancestors. The ark of the covenant is another such legacy. The ark held the stone tablets containing the Ten Commandments, which were the basis of the covenant between God and the Israelites after their flight from Egypt and during their time in the wilderness (Ex. 15:10–22). In the New Testament, Jesus spoke with a Samaritan woman at "Jacob's well" (Jn. 4:1–7). Though Jacob's well is nowhere mentioned in the Old Testament, it is clear that by the time of the writing of John's gospel, the well had taken on this tradition and had become a legacy. Can you think of other biblical legacies?

As John Ames looked ahead to his death, he started to think about the things he would leave behind. Heavy on his mind were the several boxes containing sermons he had written over the years. He estimated that he had written sixty-seven thousand, five hundred pages in the course of his career. "Pretty nearly my whole life's work is in those boxes, which is an amazing thing to reflect on…I'm a little afraid of them" (18). He was reluctant to read back through the sermons, but he did want to find some to leave for Lila and the boy. He hoped to burn the rest of them, though he noted, "It's humiliating to have written as much as Augustine, and then have to find a way to dispose of it" (40). He struggled with the question of what to do with the physical remnants of his life.

Some legacies are unwanted. When Ames I left Gilead for his final journey back to Kansas, he left a bundle of things at home. Ames remembered:

> When we learned he'd died out there, we opened it. There were some old shirts that had been white once and a few dozen sermons and some other paper wrapped with twine, and the pistol…But my father was disgusted. These things my grandfather had left were just an offense to him. So he buried them. (*Gilead*, 78–79)

After a month, however, Ames II dug the things up again. He left the gun buried in the ground, only to later dig it up again, smash it to pieces, and throw it in the river. The pistol and the bloodied shirts were painful reminders of the disappointment

Ames II found in his father, and the family was clearly at a loss about what to do with these troublesome legacies.

What legacies will the young boy have of his father? Perhaps some of his sermons will be saved after all, and he will be able to read some of his father's work. Ames promised to leave his books and hoped that the boy will find some of the notes in the margins useful. The Greek Testament, which survived so many generations, was still in the family, and so the boy will no doubt inherit that as well. On the afternoon when Ames and the boy were sitting on the porch sipping honeysuckle, Lila came out with a camera and took their picture. Those photographs will be another important reminder of John Ames's life after he is gone.

Looking Back and Looking Ahead

It is worth considering how we in the twenty-first century remember life. For those of us who communicate via e-mail, letter writing seems like an ancient art form. What form do our legacies take? What is it in our political past that defines our present and our future? World War II still looms large in our history, though eyewitnesses will soon be hard to find. The 1950s have become a period we like to remember as the good old days. The pain of Vietnam still lingers, however; that is an episode we wish we could forget. It will be interesting to see how the Iraq war will influence and shape the coming generations.

And so we return to the question with which we started this chapter: Is it better to forget or remember? Ames dearly wanted to remember precious times with his wife and son, but his father desperately wanted *not* to be reminded of Ames I's pistol and bloody shirts. About the hard times in Kansas, Ames said he agreed with his father that all is best forgotten, but did he really think so? Why, then, would he tell all this to his son? The family stories could die with him, and be forgotten. There seems, however, to be something inherently important about remembering life.

Remembering is not just about looking back; it is also about looking forward. As much as he might have thought that the past is best forgotten, remembering his past helped Ames come to terms with his present situation and helped him move forward. Didn't his abolitionist roots have something to do with his acceptance of Jack's interracial relationship? Didn't his own history of loneliness help him relate to Jack's situation? Didn't having a grandfather who fought for justice and a father who prayed for peace make him a compassionate, prayerful man? Did his father's and grandfather's opposing views on war make him simultaneously oppose World War I and sympathize with those enlisted?

We might think that remembering the past will help us change the future; maybe telling the story of the prodigal son will keep the next generation of sons from rebelling against their fathers. Given centuries of experience, however, this certainly does not seem to be the case. Even sons who know better push away their fathers in search of their own identities. Perhaps, then, we do not look to the past to avoid the mistakes of previous generations, but to accept and understand the patterns of our current relationships. Ames did not like the fact that his son made his toys into weapons, but he acknowledged that this was not a fault of this particular generation: "All children play at war now. All of them make those sounds of airplanes and bombs and crashing and exploding. We did the same things, playing at cannon fire and bayonet charges" (192). Like baseball, the details have changed, but not the game itself. No doubt tomorrow's generation will have new toys that will also be turned into guns and tanks. But we can be assured that they will also have baseball bats and catcher's mitts, and sunny afternoons.

QUESTIONS FOR DISCUSSION

1. In the mid-1950s when John Ames was writing this letter to his son, most Americans remembered World War II as the most prominent war. Why do you think Ames put such emphasis on the Civil War and made little mention of World War II?
2. Do you think Jack had any regret about the first child he fathered? Could there be any reconciliation for Jack in that situation? Did Jack's love for and care for his new wife and child make up for his previous indiscretions?
3. Jack left Gilead without telling his father about his wife and child. Do you think his journey to Gilead was in vain, or did he accomplish what he came to do?
4. *Gilead* deals with the relationships between fathers and sons. Do you think mother/daughter relationships go through the same pattern of rebellion, regret, and reconciliation? What about father/daughter or mother/son relationships?

5. Think about an important journey you have taken in your life. Were you in search of your past or your future? How did that journey serve as a bridge between the two?

For Further Reading

Thomas Goodrich, *War to the Knife: Bleeding Kansas, 1854–1861.* Mechanicsburg, Pa.: Stackpole Books, 1998.

J. Ellsworth Kalas, *Parables from the Backside*. Nashville: Abingdon Press, 1992.

Henri J. M. Nouwen, *The Return of the Prodigal Son: A Story of Homecoming*. New York: Doubleday, 1992.

Chaim Potok, *The Chosen*. New York: Simon and Schuster, 1967.

CHAPTER 5

Life of Ministry

I left you behind in Crete for this reason, so that you should put in order what remained to be done, and should appoint elders in every town, as I directed you: someone who is blameless, married only once, whose children are believers, not accused of debauchery and not rebellious. For a bishop, as God's steward, must be blameless; he must not be arrogant or quick-tempered or addicted to wine or violent or greedy for gain; but he must be hospitable, a lover of goodness, prudent, upright, devout, and self-controlled. He must have a firm grasp of the word that is trustworthy in accordance with the teaching, so that he may be able both to preach with sound doctrine and to refute those who contradict it.

(Titus 1:5–9)

There are a thousand thousand reasons to live this life, every one of them sufficient.

(Gilead, 243*)*

In the early pages of *Gilead,* Ames passed by a couple of grease monkeys smoking and joking outside the garage where they worked. As the young men saw the minister approach, their joking stopped.

> That's the strangest thing about this life, about being in the ministry. People change the subject when they see you coming. And then sometimes those very same people come into your study and tell you the most remarkable things. There's a lot under the surface of life, everyone knows that. A lot of malice and dread and guilt, and so much loneliness, where you wouldn't really expect to find it, either. (*Gilead,* 6)

A minister's life is a peculiar one. Ministers are privy to the deepest and darkest recesses of another person's soul. Yet, they are denied access to the parts of that same person's life that are laid bare to a world of strangers. A minister's personal friends may choose to keep vital details of their lives secret, yet a total stranger will pour out their most personal hopes, dreams, and fears. As we saw in chapter 2, many denominations require ministers to undergo a rigorous education process, including dead languages and heavy theological concepts. They might spend much time in study; we saw the rigors and depth of Ames's thinking on the issue of Jack alone. Yet, ministers must have facility with the day-to-day concerns of life: plumbing, illness, and how to spruce up a church's exterior.

In the previous chapter, we looked at the father/son relationships in *Gilead,* and considered how rebellion, regret, and attempts at reconciliation characterize them. Some readers might be surprised that a family with so many ministers could contain so much contention. You might ask yourself, "Shouldn't ministers rise above those concerns that plague other people?" Recall the conflict between Ames's father and grandfather: "In a spirit of Christian forgiveness very becoming to men of the cloth, and to father and son, they had buried their differences. It must be said, however, that they buried them not very deeply, and perhaps more as one would bank a fire than smother it" (34).

Gilead provides a glimpse into the interior life of one minister, revealing Ames to be an ordinary man, subject to the same desires, limitations, and frustrations that confound those to whom he ministers. Being a minister steeped in a life of faith does not protect Ames from pain and sorrow. What may distinguish Ames, however, is the way he reflects upon the events of the day and the feelings of his heart. Reconciliation with Jack isn't just a desirable goal, but a cause for examining the deepest parts of his Christian faith and church tradition. Water isn't merely a resource for cleanliness and sustenance; it is a sign of God's blessing.

In this chapter we will explore the concept of "minister," looking at "ministers" in the Bible, and then at Ames's life as a minister in Gilead. We'll pay particular attention to the sermon process, and also to the two most important sources of support Ames enjoys: his wife, Lila, and old friend Boughton.

Ministers in the Bible: Priests, Prophets, Bishops and Deacons

Think of all the tasks that a minister performs: preaching, counseling, marrying, burying, baptizing, teaching, and leading worship. These functions are not unique to the Judeo-Christian tradition, nor are they things only a twenty-first–century minister does. Throughout history, in every religion in the world, societies have had specially appointed people to mediate worship of a higher divinity, interpret divine mandates and actions, articulate divine wishes, educate and initiate people into the faith, and shepherd people through life's transitions.

In the Judeo-Christian tradition, "ministry" started with the priesthood. This priesthood evolved over time, from the earliest days until the time of Christ. The Christian Testament uses other terms for "minister." In the *New Revised Standard Version* we see the terms "apostles," "deacons," "elders," "bishops," and so forth. Their duties aren't clearly defined, but their qualifications are, as we shall see.

Ministers in the Old Testament

When we think of a minister, we might think of service to people. But in the Old Testament, priests were to be of service to God:

> But the levitical priests, the descendants of Zadok, who kept the charge of my sanctuary when the people of Israel went astray from me, shall come near to me to minister to me; and they shall attend me to offer me the fat and the blood says the Lord GOD. It is they who shall enter my sanctuary, it is they who shall approach my table, to minister to me, and they shall keep my charge. (Ezek. 44:15–16)

In the time of the patriarchs (see chapter 2), there was no specific priesthood. The head of the family often carried out priestly duties, such as offering sacrifices to God. The early Israelites were a nomadic, tribal people. Moses functioned as a priest for the emerging nation (Ex. 24:1–8; compare 2:16–22). As the society grew more structured and settled, the separate class of "priests" developed, particularly as temples were established. According to the book of Deuteronomy, God set aside the family of one of Jacob's sons, Levi, for the priesthood (Deut. 10:8–9; compare 33:8–11). They apparently functioned during the wilderness wanderings (Num. 3:21–37; 10:17, 21) and were divided into three branches—Gershonites, Kohathites, and Merarites (Ex. 6:16). The book of Exodus designates Moses' brother, Aaron, and his sons, who were of the tribe of Levi, as priests (Ex. 28:41; 29:7; 30:30; 40:13, 15; Lev. 7:36;

8:12; Num. 3:3). Under Joshua, levitical priests carried the ark (Josh. 3:3; 6:4–20; 8:30–35).

In the period of the Judges, temples dotted the land of Canaan from north to south (see temple at Dan, Judg. 18:7; at Bethel, 20:18–27). Levitical priests were the only ones who could perform sacrifices and other functions at the temples, even though non-priests sacrificed on altars or other special places. The Levites had no land and depended on sacrifices for food (Deut. 18:1–15; Josh. 13:14, 33; 14:3–4; 18:30) but were highly honored (Judg. 17:7–13). Some apparently lived in the country away from the cities and had to depend on charity (Deut. 12:11–12, 18; 14:25–27; 16:11; 18:6–8; 26:2). At least some of the Levites ministered at the central sanctuary, giving divine oracles with Urim and Thummim (Deut. 17:9, 12; 19:17; 20:2; 21:5; 24:8). They taught Moses' law (Deut. 17:18; 27:9–10; 31:9–11, 24–26) and conducted the rituals connected with the ark (Deut. 10:7–8; 31:9, 25). They also sacrificed and received offerings (Deut. 18:1, 3; 26:4).

Eventually under David and then Josiah, worship was centralized in Jerusalem, and all the priests served there. Solomon banished Abiathar and made Zadok the chief priest. Later, Aaron's descendants served as primary priests, while other Levites held secondary roles such as musicians and gatekeepers (1 Chr. 15:17–24; 16:4–7, 25; 25—26). In the north Jeroboam I created a non-levitic priesthood (1 Kings 12:31).

After the exile, the priesthood came to dominate the nation of Israel. The head of the temple was automatically the head of the Judean government, and his duties included diplomacy and collecting taxes, along with spiritual matters. Then, when Herod became King of Judea, the priests lost much of their political power.

Israel's law included complex religious purity laws, many of which concerned sanitary and hygienic conditions. The priests helped maintain the distinction between what was pure and what wasn't. They diagnosed leprosy and performed purification rites. Priests also performed sacrifices and offerings, which ensured good relations between God and the people. Priests pronounced blessings on individuals and on the nation. They blew trumpets on festive occasions, maintained the temple, and collected donations and tithes. They taught the law, or the Torah, to the people, and also helped interpret it. Priests were subject to special purity laws. For example, they couldn't officiate if they were ritually impure and could only marry a virgin of Israel. A priest could not go to a cemetery except for the burial of his closest relatives.

Besides Aaron, other prominent priests in the early period included Phinehas of Bethel (Judg. 20:28) and Eleazar (Josh. 19:51; 21:1) and Eli, both priests at Shiloh, where the ark of the covenant was located. Eli blessed the barren Hannah after she prayed to God for a child. Hannah then conceived the child Samuel, who would follow in Eli's footsteps. The early monarchy knew such priests as Ahijah, Zadok, and Abiathar (1 Sam. 22:11–23; 30:7; 2 Sam. 8:17). Later we hear of Ahimaaz, Azariah (I), Johanan, Azariah (II), Amariah (II), Ahitub (II), Zadok (II), Shallum, Hilkiah, Azariah (III), Seraiah, and Jehozadak (1 Chr. 6:1–15).

We might also consider as "ministers" the many prophets of the Old Testament, such as Elijah and Ezekiel. A "prophet" delivered divine messages to groups or individuals. We might think of them as forecasting the future, but it would be more accurate to describe prophets as informing people of moral and ethical duties. In good times, prophets warned the people to obey God, forecasting doom if the people did not. In bad times, prophets might offer hope, promises of better times ahead, or explanations as to why the people's fortunes had turned. Today, for many people, the mark of a good preacher is whether he or she is "prophetic." Recall Ames's lament:

> I woke up this morning thinking this town might as well be standing on the absolute floor of hell for all the truth there is in it and the fault is mine as much as anyone's. I was thinking about the things that had happened here just in my lifetime—the droughts and the influenza and the Depression and three terrible wars. It seems to me now we never looked up from the trouble we had just getting by to put the obvious question, that is, to ask what it was the Lord was trying to make us understand. The word "preacher" comes form an old French word, *predicateur,* which means prophet. And what is the purpose of a prophet except to find meaning in trouble. (*Gilead,* 233)

Ministers in the New Testament

The most common word for "minister" in the Christian Testament is the Greek word *diakonos,* or deacon. Depending on one's denomination, that might be misleading when considering how we understand the roles of ordained clergy and deacons.

A number of terms are used for ministers in the New Testament. In the book of Acts, the eleven remaining disciples must find a replacement for Judas. They pray about which of two candidates should "take the place in this ministry and apostleship" (Acts 1:25).

Later in Acts, the twelve "apostles" must solve the problem of widows being neglected. They "called together the whole community of the disciples and said, 'it is not right that we should neglect the word of God in order to wait on tables. Therefore, friends, select from among yourselves seven men of good standing, full of the Spirit and of wisdom, whom we may appoint to this task, while we, for our part, will devote ourselves to prayer and to serving the word'"(6:2–4). These seven are considered the first "deacons."

Yet the duties of those seven go far beyond waiting on tables. Stephen "did great wonders and signs among the people" (6:8), preached, and eventually was martyred (see Acts 7). Our modern "Stephen Ministry," in which lay members of a congregation learn to provide pastoral care for others, is named after this Stephen. Phillip, another of the seven, preached in Samaria and baptized the Ethiopian eunuch (see Acts 8).

Paul listed a number of ministries in his letters: apostles, prophets, teachers, healers, helpers, miracle workers, those who speak in tongues, and pastors. Paul seemed to put the ministerial roles in some kind of order, with apostles being "first." The writer of 1 Timothy seemed to hold up preachers and teachers for double honor (1 Tim. 5:17).

In the greeting to the church in Philippi, Paul mentioned "bishops" (or "overseers"), as well as deacons. He described bishops' and deacons' qualifications in 1 Timothy 1–13, much as in his letter to Titus (see introduction to this chapter). He did not, however, describe their duties.

But in his letter to the Ephesians, Paul wrote that the work of ministers was "to equip the saints for the work of ministry, for building up the body of Christ, until all of us come to the unity of the faith and of the knowledge of the Son of God, to maturity, to the measure of the full stature of Christ" (Eph. 4:12–13). He wrote that ministers of all kinds were necessary to teach and lead Christ's followers. The overwhelming message of the New Testament is that all followers of Christ are to perform ministerial roles: A teacher is as much a minister as a preacher; a healer is as much a minister as a prophet.

You may have heard the term "priesthood of all believers," which is one of the distinctive ideas associated with the Protestant reformation. Rather than needing an ordained person to mediate our relationship with God, each person has direct access to Christ.

We are all worthy to pray to God for ourselves and for other people. Each person is also called to be a "servant" to all people. We don't have to wait for an ordained clergy person to lift up prayers for the sick or to visit the elderly in a nursing home. Each of us "saints" is equipped to be a minister. Part of the job of the ordained clergy is to equip the saints to perform ministry.

A Minister's Life in Gilead

A minister may be called many things: clergy; person of the cloth; reverend; priest; preacher. The word *minister* is from a Latin word that means servant. The word *pastor* derives from the Latin term for "herdsman" or "shepherd." The term *reverend* is actually a title or description. It, too, comes from a Latin word meaning "worthy of being revered." Many churches refer to their leader as "preacher," even though she or he also performs the many other functions of a minister, such as teaching, providing care, and so on.

Indeed, Ames performed many functions in his church. He seemed to take particular delight in baptizing infants, in the intellectual rigors of preparing sermons, and in conferring with his flock. But he also attended deaths, prayed for people, and was even called on to fix plumbing problems.

The relationship between a congregation and its minister is a peculiar animal. Ames was an employee in that the congregation compensated him for performing certain duties. Yet the role was beyond hired hand. Typically, a church does not "hire" a minister, but "calls" a minister. The relationship is a covenantal one in which mutual care is expected. Ames's congregation cared for him during his single years by bringing him casseroles and stews (120), and by attempting to find him a suitable mate (55). This particular congregation provided him a parsonage, which is a house provided for the minister's use. Upkeep is typically provided by the congregation, which owns the house.

In return, Ames gave generously of his meager salary. At times he paid for windowpanes and paint for the church, things we might expect to come from the church's coffers. Ames was keenly aware that the church's coffers were supplied from the pockets of parishioners. In lean years, he was sensitive to the strain such items would put, not on an impersonal church budget, but on his flock.

Ames seemed particularly sensitive to many aspects of life. As we noted in chapter 3, Ames was aware of the beauty of the daily happenings and common people who populated his life. The recollection of playing catch brought back the remembrance of "that wonderful collaboration of the whole body with itself and that wonderful certainty and amazement when you know the glove is just where it should be" (115). Even an "ordinary Sunday" is an occasion for a poetic reflection on the "silent and invisible life" (20).

Ames was especially attuned to the yin-yang aspects of life. Every good and beautiful thing carried an edge of sorrow. Every tragedy bore an element of beauty. Hardship yielded to blessing; blessing carried hardship. Of the women singing hymns with their hair undone after the church fire, he wrote, "it was so joyful and sad" (96). Of baptizing the woman who would become his wife, Ames wrote: "I could hardly bring myself to touch the water to her brow because she looked a good deal more than beautiful. Sadness was a great part of it, it was" (93). Sorrow itself was beautiful: "I believe there is a dignity in sorrow simply because it is God's good pleasure that there should be. He is forever raising up those who are brought low" (137). Of Boughton's large, healthy family he writes, "good fortune is not only good fortune" (65). Of his infant daughter's death: "the worst misfortune isn't only misfortune" (56).

Perhaps appreciating the yin-yang aspects of life is a minister's greatest task. The point is not to see a silver lining in the bad times, or to provide a reality check for the good. Rather, the task is to help people see that the workings of God are beyond simple conceptions of "good" and "bad." The minister teaches that even in times of tragedy, God is at work, and that the mystery of a life of faith carries a pathos that comes from the "not yet" aspect of Christianity, which hopes in joy and confidence for a better tomorrow.

Preaching a Word

A good sermon, wrote John Ames, "is one side of a passionate conversation" among three parties: the preacher, the congregation, and God (45). Not only are these three present in the Sunday morning delivery, but also during the sermon preparation. Scripture must be balanced with real life; Ames's thoughts must be balanced with scripture and with the needs of the congregation. Any of the three parties—God (including God's word as revealed in the Bible), the congregation, or Ames's own thought process—might be the starting point for a sermon.

Ames used to make his way through the Bible in orderly fashion. "Now, though, I talk about whatever is on my mind—Hagar and Ishmael at the moment" (118). At other times, the concerns of the congregation were at the forefront of Ames's sermon preparation. "There have always been things I felt I must tell them, even if no one listened or understood" (144). Either way, Ames's sermons were anchored in the Bible.

In his book *They Like to Never Quit Praisin' God* (Cleveland: United Church Press, 1997), minister Frank Thomas describes a sermon as the intersection of two "streets": life and scripture. A minister writing a sermon seeking to resonate with a congregation's experience begins either on the street of life and continues along until he meets the road of scripture, or he begins on a road of scripture and continues until he comes to the street of life. We see this in Ames's sermon preparation:

> The story of Hagar and Ishmael came to mind while I was praying this morning, and I found a great assurance in it. The story says that it is not only the father of a child who cares for its life, who protects its mother, and it says that even if the mother can't find a way to provide for it, or herself, provision will be made. (*Gilead*, 118–19)

Ames was very concerned in his own life about the welfare of his wife and child after his death, as he had made no financial provision for survivors. He would take comfort in the portion of the Hagar-Ishmael story in which God provided for them in the wilderness. In delivering the sermon, the elderly Ames noted "the children of old age are unspeakably precious" (129). But each person reads scripture through the lens of his or her own experience. The story of fathers and children rang far differently in the ears of Jack Boughton as he sat in the pew. Based on his own tragic experiences with children, and his questioning of God's grace for him, the story of Hagar and Ishmael may have caused him to feel guilty.

As a person's life changes, so will the outlook on scripture and the understanding of truth. Throughout his ministry, Ames spent much time in study and deep theological reflection. He meant every word of every sermon he wrote—at least he did *at the time* he wrote it (40). From the vantage point of near death, however, Ames recognized that his outlook and appreciation of the world had changed through the years.

Perhaps this is why he was so preoccupied with the boxes of sermons in the attic. While they represented his life's work and the fruit of many hours of careful, rigorous thought, he recognized that his view of life at the time he wrote many of them was somewhat myopic. He also recognized that in the three-way conversation of the sermonic moment, his voice may have been the loudest: "I hope I was speaking to them, not only to myself, as it seems to me sometimes when I look back" (41).

Ames recognized the danger in relying too heavily on imperfect human reasoning. There is a truth that eludes our earthly understanding but will be revealed on our death, he believed. So he imagined his dead daughter listening to his sermons:

> That was a sort of trick I played on myself, to keep from taking doctrines and controversies too much to heart. I read so many books in those days, and I was always disputing in my mind with one or another of them, but I think I usually knew better than to take too much of that sort of thing into the pulpit. (*Gilead,* 20)

A minister must find a point of contact between his resources and real life. It is not a positive sign that a parishioner had to ask, "Who is Feuerbach?" (143). To be useful as a ministerial resource, a theologian's work must ultimately resonate in the events of life. It is the minister's job to stand with one foot in the world of scholarship and the other in the world of ordinary life. The most profound theology in the world will not resonate with a congregation if it remains in the abstract.

Moreover, a preacher must be ever mindful of how a congregation will understand his sermon. It is one thing to express your thoughts, interpretations, and feelings. It is quite another to be on the receiving end of that expression. For the most part, Ames balanced his desire and calling to express a prophetic message with the timeliness and appropriateness of that message. Ames recalled in particular the sermon he never preached about World War I. Ames's grandfather had "preached his people into the war" (101); Ames wished he could preach them away from war. In this sermon, Ames identified the epidemic of Spanish influenza as a warning sign against the Great War. Instead of preaching the sermon, he burned it.

> It was quite a sermon, I believe...But my courage failed, because I knew the only people at church would be a few old women who were already about as sad and apprehensive as they could stand to be and no more approving of the war than I was...I wish I had kept it, because I meant every word. It might have been the only sermon I wouldn't

> mind answering for in the next world. And I burned it. But Mirabelle Mercer was not Pontius Pilate, and she was not Woodrow Wilson, either. (*Gilead*, 42–43)

Women in Ministry in Gilead

One sunny, Sunday afternoon in Kansas City, Missouri, a large African American congregation installed its new minister. The service included two sermons, a full gospel choir, and lots of prayers. After the benediction, the young minister was seated at the front of the sanctuary, and next to him was his wife, each in a large upholstered chair. The couple greeted their new flock as they filed past.

The young wife was boldly introduced as the congregation's "first lady," to be afforded the same respect as the minister. As a full partner in her husband's ministry, she would have duties and obligations to fulfill, as well as expectations of decorum and wisdom to meet. In a number of African American churches, as well as some white churches, a minister's spouse is understood to be part of a ministry team. In other churches, a minister's spouse must make it abundantly clear to the congregation what his or her level of involvement will be.

Female spouses, in particular, who do not intend to be part of fellowship groups, cook for pot-luck dinners, teach Sunday school, or clean the church kitchen could be bucking generations of congregational tradition. And even in progressive churches in which a clergy spouse is not expected for special duty, a congregation still tends to cast a watchful eye over a minister's spouse and children.

We see in *Gilead* the pressures that Lila Ames endured. People assumed she could not cook and continued to deliver food to the family. She was worried about her poor grammar and her lack of religious background. She was reluctant to reveal her past, which apparently included poverty, sorrow, and a lifestyle unbecoming to a minister's wife of the mid-1950s. When Jack offered her a cigarette, Lila declined:

> "No, Thank you." She laughed. "Sure I would. It just isn't seemly in a preacher's wife."
>
> " 'It just isn't seemly'! I guess they've been after you."
>
> "I don't mind," she said. "Somebody had to tell me a few things sooner or later. Now I been seemly so long I'm almost beginning to like it." (*Gilead*, 199)

As a minister is a figure of "celebrity" and authority, a minister's family bears more responsibility and duty, much like the family of a president. We can also look to the Bible to understand the additional expectations of a clergy family. The biblical "household codes" (see for example Col. 3:18–22; 4:1 and Eph. 5:21—6:9, among other passages) typically place wives in subordination to their husbands. Add to this Paul's qualification for a bishop: "He must manage his own household well, keeping his children submissive and respectful in every way—for if someone does not know how to manage his own household, how can he take care of God's church?" (1 Tim. 3:4–5). A minister's family can reflect either favorably or poorly on the minister.

Ames was concerned about the relationship between Lila and the congregation:

> Then, when your mother and I got married, it was a little hard for people to learn that they couldn't just come and go anymore. They suspected she was not a cook, I believe, and in fact she was not, so they kept coming in the door with their casseroles until I realized it upset her, and then I spoke with them about it. I found her crying in the pantry one evening. Someone had come in and changed the pull cord on the light and put new paper down on the shelves. It was kindly intended but not considerate. I understand that. (*Gilead,* 121)

Of course, not all clergy spouses are women. As more and more women enter the ordained ministry, more men find themselves in the role of clergy spouse. We might ask ourselves whether clergy husbands are held to the same expectations as clergy wives, and whether the children of female clergy are held to the same standards as children of male clergy.

Women have been in the ordained ministry for more than a century, but all the ordained ministers in *Gilead* are men. Yet the women in their lives do more than merely meet, or attempt to meet, expectations of the community. They are in their own ways ministers, acting where the ordained ministers will not or cannot:

Louisa—During Ames's childhood, while many children trembled in fear of a rumored murderer, Louisa "said we ought to pray for the man's conversion. Her thought was that it would be better to go to the source of the problem than to keep praying for divine intervention on behalf of each one of us in every situation of possible danger" (83). The thought of praying for the mythical murderer never occurred to either Boughton or Ames, who would later become ministers.

Glory—The Boughton family was dismayed at the condition in which Jack's daughter lived. But Glory took the initiative to provide for the child, to drive Mr. and Mrs. Boughton and Ames to see her, and even to formulate a plan to rescue her. Glory seemed to be the most deeply moved: "Glory used to come to me and cry about it, because nothing ever got better" (157).

Lila Ames—During the front-porch debate about predestination (see chapter 2), the ministers seemed to dance around the subject and offer Jack no satisfying answers. Ames suspected Jack had ulterior motives. But Lila identified Jack's real question: "But your mother spoke up, which surprised us all. She said, 'What about being saved?' She said, 'If you can't change, there don't seem much purpose in it'" (152). She finally delivered the answer Jack had been seeking: "Your mother said, 'A person can change. Everything can change'" (153). On the way home, she rebuked her husband for being so harsh with Jack. Lila was also able to bless Jack, when Ames could not (200), and while Ames only thought abstractly about all the sermons in the attic, Lila actually went through them, picking out a few for Ames himself (160).

Mrs. Martha Ames (II)—When Ames's father and grandfather approached the point of fighting, Martha Ames intervened: "'It's Sunday. It's the Lord's Day. It's the Sabbath,'" (83). After Ames's grandfather died, she insisted that the old man's effects be handled properly. She scrubbed his shirts as clean as possible, carefully ironed and folded them, and then buried them as if burying the old man himself (81). She was the only one to speak to the old man after his Fourth of July speech (176). Caught between the eccentric old man and his hotheaded son, Martha Ames kept the house on a practical, loving, even keel.

Mrs. Margaret Ames (I)—We know very little about Mrs. Ames I, only that she suffered a harsh life, being married to a minister who was willing to sacrifice everything for the cause of the abolition. She was sickly and unable to care properly for her children, but got no sympathy from her fiery husband (89–90). Yet her loyalty to him caused her to attend church when her son began worshiping with the Quakers, in spite of her profound pain and deteriorating condition (193).

Della—Jack's spirited and loving common-law wife caused him to face up to certain aspects of his life and personality, and to summon courage to approach her imposing minister father. Jack admitted, "Though I can now say that the influence of my wife worked a change in me for the better, at least temporarily" (222).

Ames regretted his inability to reconcile with Jack in his heart. The women of *Gilead* seem to be stronger in this respect than the men, and perhaps that is why they sometimes seem more pastoral than the minister men:

> It is one of the best traits of good people that they love where they pity. And this is truer of women than of men. So they get themselves drawn into situations that are harmful to them. I have seen this happen many, many times. I have always had trouble finding a way to caution against it. Since it is, in a word, Christlike. (*Gilead*, 186–87)

A Friend in Need: The Blessing of a Clergy Colleague

In the Gilgamesh epic of ancient Babylon, the lonely hero-giant Gilgamesh has no one like himself on Earth. To ease his suffering, the gods give him a friend, a companion and playmate named Enkidu. Some Old Testament scholars compare this ancient myth with the story of Adam and Eve. In Genesis, God says, "It is not good that the man should be alone; I will make him a helper as his partner" (Gen. 2:18). In the Bible, God gives Adam a woman as a "helper"; in the Gilgamesh epic, the gods give Gilgamesh a buddy.

We all need somebody with whom we can share the unique nature of our inner struggles; we need someone in our lives who is like we are. Lila provided Ames with a sympathetic ear, companionship, wisdom, and partnership. But spouses are not intended to fill a person's every need. Boughton and Ames relied on each other's friendship, wisdom, and companionship throughout their lives.

Ames and Boughton had spent many days together in rowdy boyhood, walking on stilts, covertly assembling a hay wagon on the courthouse roof, and wondering together how life would turn out. The two had seen each other through many of life's transitions, up to and including their mutual anticipation of the latest transition into what follows earthly life.

As friends, Boughton and Ames exhibited their respect and duty to one another. When Ames was away during the premature birth of his daughter, Boughton stepped in and baptized her, choosing the name "Angeline" from a favorite scripture. Likewise, Ames baptized Jack. As colleagues in ministry, the two translated scripture together, conferred with each other in pastoral care issues, and prayed for each other's flock.

The relationship between Boughton and Ames was deeper than normal friendship or collegiality. The ministers held each other in a unique and privileged place, sharing with each other what they shared with no one else: "I've spent a good share of my life comforting the afflicted, but I could never endure the thought that anyone should try to comfort me, except old Boughton, who always knew better than to talk much. He was such an excellent friend to me in those days, such a help to me" (40).

Their mutual fatherhood for Jack reveals the depth of their feeling for each other. Tears rolled down Boughton's face as he revealed his infant son would bear the name of his friend. Ames's resistance and resentment didn't diminish the significance of the gift, though the significance seemed to elude Ames. "Boughton named him for me because he thought he might not have another son and I most likely would not have any child at all. It was very kind of him" (87). Likewise, Ames is protective of his dear friend: "Jack has grieved his father terribly…and I have only grieved Boughton myself when he has felt I was slow to forgive Jack, too" (189).

Just as the existence of Jack created a special bond between the two ministers, it also proved a source of tension. Boughton was delighted over Jack's homecoming, while Ames was suspicious. Ames had shared Boughton's family's distress over Jack for years. He knew about Jack's teenage antics and about the baby Jack sired. Eventually, Boughton shared the depth of his concern for Jack with his friend, "and we sat there together and talked and prayed, about John Ames Boughton, for John Ames Boughton" (121). Ames's ambivalence about Jack and his protective love for his friend made it difficult for him to know how to respond to Jack's arrival: "If there is one thing I don't want to do in the time that remains to either one of us, it is offend Boughton" (148).

The presence of a friend and colleague is especially important for clergy. Beyond having in common the peculiarities of a life of ministry, ministers process the events of life in unique ways. It would not be satisfying for Ames to simply "unload" all the worries and frustrations on a casual acquaintance or even his wife. Ames thought deeply and theologically about everyday matters, and

Boughton was a capable and inviting conversation partner. The two talked at length about the subject of baptism, and even that "there is nothing more astonishing than a human face" (66).

The deep and abiding friendship between Boughton and Ames was a reliable resource, both in the daily ups and downs of life, during times of celebration, and in particularly difficult times. Each saw in the other truths that escaped the perceptions of others, even their families. "When I look at Boughton, I see a funny, generous young man, full of vigor. He's on two canes now, and he says if he could sprout a third arm there would be three" (118).

The Harder Parts of Ministry

> You can spend forty years teaching people to be awake to the fact of mystery and then some fellow with no more theological sense than a jackrabbit gets himself a radio ministry and all your work is forgotten. (*Gilead*, 208)

Such is the frustration of a lifelong congregational minister. We have spent much of this chapter examining the joyful aspects of a minister's life: sermon preparation, a loving congregation, a devoted spouse, and a trusted friend. But a minister's life is not easy. A clerical vocation does not protect a person from fear, anger, sorrow, or rage. In fact, a minister is often more likely to feel these emotions because of a keener sensitivity and passion and because of the life events a minister encounters. At the same time, people expect that a minister can "handle" things better than other people.

Like a psychotherapist, a minister is exposed daily to other people's worries and anxieties. She or he is involved routinely in some of the most stressful aspects of life: births, illness, death, divorce, failures, marriage, successes. Even positive transitions, such as new parenthood or a new career, are times of high stress. At the same time, clergy are among the lowest-paid professionals, despite heavy requirements for education and time commitments. On average, clergy earn significantly less than teachers, therapists, funeral directors, nurses, and emergency workers such as police and firefighters.

Among Ames's biggest regrets is the lack of financial resources to support his family after his death. A minister makes little money, and, if he lives in a parsonage, his home is not his own. Ames grieves the hardship the boy and Lila will face without the family breadwinner, and possibly without the parsonage, which will likely be the home of the next minister. "I do regret that I have almost nothing to leave you and your mother…I never made any money to speak of, and I never paid any attention to the money I had. It was the furthest thing from my mind that I'd be leaving a wife and child, believe me. I'd have been a better father if I'd known. I'd have set something by for you" (4).

Additionally, a minister encounters perhaps the most difficult questions of life: Why does my brother have cancer? Why did a tornado hit our home? What awaits me after this life? Should I tell my family I'm gay? Should I continue life support for my grandmother? Should this country go to war?

Such questions have no definitive answers, at least not easy ones. It is not necessarily a minister's place to provide solid answers in the face of life mysteries. A minister can only help a person discern what God is doing in any given situation. Yet providing comfort can override the reluctance to give answers.

> I don't know how many times people have asked me what death is like…people as old as I am now would ask me, hold onto my hands and look into my eyes with their old milky eyes, as if they knew I knew and they were going to *make* me tell them. I used to say it was like going home. (*Gilead,* 3–4)

Perhaps no questions vexed Ames more than questions about the truth of faith. There are two parts to his frustration. First, any attempt to prove the mysteries of life and matters of faith would be woefully inadequate: "I think the attempt to defend belief can unsettle it, in fact, because there is always an inadequacy in argument about ultimate things" (178). Perhaps this was why he refuses to try to convince Jack about Christianity.

> You might think I am under some sort of obligation to try to "save" young Boughton, that by inquiring into these things he is putting me under that obligation. Well, I have had a certain amount of experience with skepticism and the conversation it generates, and there is an inevitable futility in it. It is even destructive. (*Gilead,* 176–77)

Second, Ames seemed to suspect that such inquiries were insincere: "It seems to me some people just go around looking to get their faith unsettled. That has been the fashion for the last hundred years or so" (24). Engaging in these conversations set Ames up in an impossible position of defense: "And they want me to defend religion, and they want me to give them 'proofs.' I just won't do it. It only confirms them in their skepticism" (177).

There is much truth in Ames's conclusion that, in defending the divine mysteries of life, argument is futile. Indeed, many "questions" posed by people who claim to have no faith or who are exploring faith aren't really questions at all. In many cases, the questioner has already made up his or her mind that faith is bunk. In these instances, any "proof" that might be provided would be refuted, disregarded, or disputed; no amount of evidence would ever be sufficient.

But all people of all faiths—not just clergy—would do well to keep open minds regarding inquiries into their beliefs. We are all called to be ministers, and part of a minister's role is to educate others about our faith. Much misunderstanding among world religions comes not only from a reluctance to ask questions, but also from a disposition not to answer them, either. Asking real questions is healthy. Answers are not presumed to be known, and inquiry is sincere. In addition, when we are asked questions about our faith, we have the opportunity to think more deeply about what we believe and why we believe it, even if we are unsure of our answers.

No longer is one religion so prevalent that we can assume people know its basic tenets. No longer do most people go to a worship service in which they would learn about faith. The many well-intended seekers in the world deserve honest answers when inquiring into matters of faith, even when the answer is simply, "I don't know."

The Changing Face of Ministry

The practice and profession of ministry have changed considerably in the half-century since Ames served his flock in Gilead, Iowa. One of the biggest changes is the presence of more and more women in the pulpit. Many congregations are finding women ministers possess special gifts and sensitivities.

Other changes in ministry similarly reflect changes in society. Once a church could rely on volunteers to carry out much of its mission, but today's schedules are more demanding, with women in the workforce, children's involvement in organized activities, and work weeks that might encompass seventy or eighty hours. People's concerns are shifting as well, and ministers are being called on to guide people in care for their earth, nation, and communities, as well as each other.

Many in the younger generations are less likely to view a minister as an authoritative, all-knowing figure who deserves automatic respect and deference. Baby Boomers have been taught to "question authority" and to reexamine basic values and rules for living that their parents merely assumed to be correct. Additionally, a number of high-profile clergy persons have been exposed as agents of scandal, malfeasance, and adultery.

For their part, ministers might not be as likely to wrap themselves as completely in the life of the congregation as their predecessors. Clergy are realizing that healthy ministry relies on a healthy minister, and a healthy ministerial lifestyle includes adequate rest, recreation, reflection, and assistance from either paid staff or lay volunteers. This does not mean a minister is not as deeply involved in church life or as emotionally invested in it. But the more ministers care appropriately for themselves, the more ministers have to offer to others.

Perhaps in your own religious experience you have noticed an evolution in the way your clergyperson functions. As God continues to work in the world, unfolding new opportunities and new ways of experiencing God's good creation, God will continue to call all kinds of people to be caretakers for God's people. God will also continue to reveal new and exciting ways these ministers can serve the world, protecting those people and those things that are vulnerable, and drawing God's children ever closer into the divine embrace.

QUESTIONS FOR DISCUSSION

1. What do you think when you hear the word *minister*? Is a minister necessarily an ordained person? Are your attitudes and beliefs about ordained clergy similar to those expressed by the citizens of the fictional town of Gilead? How are they the same? How are they different?
2. This chapter discussed the life of ministry of John Ames III. He practiced a very different style of ministry than his grandfather and father. How would you characterize the ministries of all three men?
3. How do the ministries described in the Bible, the ministries described in *Gilead*, and the ministries you have experienced differ? How are they the same?

4. Do you agree with the concept of "a priesthood of all believers"? If so, why would we need ordained clergy at all? What function does an ordained clergyperson have that a layperson does not?
5. Do you have a personal relationship with a minister? What do you expect the minister to do for you? What responsibilities do you feel you have for the minister?

For Further Reading

Georges Bernanos, *Diary of a Country Priest*. New York: Carroll & Graf Publishers, 2002.

Fred C. Craddock, *Preaching*. Nashville: Abingdon Press, 1985.

Kenneth C. Haugk, *Christian Caregiving: A Way of Life*. Minneapolis: Augsburg, 1984.

Richard Lischer, *Open Secrets: A Spiritual Journey through a Country Church*. New York: Doubleday, 2001.

Barbara Brown Taylor, *The Preaching Life*. Cambridge, Mass.: Cowley Publications, 1993.

Frank Thomas, *They Like to Never Quit Praisin' God* (Cleveland: United Church Press, 1997).

CHAPTER 6

Life as Blessing

The Lord *bless you and keep you;*
the Lord *make his face to shine upon you, and be gracious to you;*
the Lord *lift up his countenance upon you, and give you peace.*

(Num. 6:24–26)

There is a reality in blessing, which I take baptism to be, primarily. It doesn't enhance sacredness, but it acknowledges it, and there is a power in that.

(Gilead, 23)

In a small, country church, a new mother carried her infant son to the front of the congregation, her husband and two daughters following behind. The minister took the baby in her arms, telling the congregation what a blessing the tiny one was to them. She told the beaming parents what a blessing they would be to their new son. With the side of her thumb, she drew a cross on the forehead of the baby, repeating words of blessing from Numbers 6.

Two young women stood next to the moving truck they had just spent two days packing. An atlas lay on the front seat, a cooler of snacks and drinks sat on the floor. Only two days before they had received their bachelor's degrees, and now they were ready to strike out on their own. Standing with the new college graduates were parents, siblings, friends, and an aunt. The group joined hands, and one by one asked for God's blessing on the trip and upon the women's new careers.

A middle-aged couple stood on their new floor of raw plywood, breathed the smell of sawdust, and admired the two-by-four frame that would become a built-in entertainment center. Soon, their friend Mark arrived, and they showed him where their big-screen television would go. Walking around saws and sawhorses, they pointed out the rooms where Janet's mother would live, the special countertops, the curved windows. And then they stood in the center of the house and sighed. Mark smiled at the couple and said, "May this new home be a sanctuary for you, a place of God's peace and protection."

During times of transition, many call on God to bless the occasion with participation, protection, approval, or divine seal. We call on God to bless new babies, the ill, the newly married, the recently widowed. We ask God to bless our meals, to bless people who do us favors, to bless those who sneeze. We call on God to bless baseball games, new sailing vessels, racetracks.

Through storytelling, use of resources, prayer, remembrances, and practicing ministry, all of life can, indeed, be a blessing to each of us. Even as he faced death, Ames recognized divine mystery wending its way through sorrow, hardship, despair, and disappointment. In the previous chapter we discussed some of Ames's joys as a minister. Among his favorites was conferring a blessing, baptism in particular:

> The sensation is of really knowing a creature, I mean really feeling its mysterious life and your own mysterious life at the same time. I don't wish to be urging the ministry on you, but there are some advantages to it you might not know to take account of if I did not point them out. Not that you have to be a minister to confer a blessing. You are simply much more likely to find yourself in that position. It's a thing people expect of you. (*Gilead*, 23)

Ames was correct in that one need not be a clergyperson—a minister, imam, rabbi, or lama—to bless something or someone. Ancient tradition, however, would indicate that clergy are somehow special agents for God's blessing. When clergy are present, we usually look to them to confer blessings.

Besides the distinction of his ordination, Ames also seemed particularly attuned to God's mystery. He was able to recognize blessing where others may not have. Two grease monkeys hanging around outside a garage are a source of beauty; a couple standing under a rain-drenched branch are recipients of blessing; the sight of sun and moon on opposite horizons are a sign of God's approval of a deed accomplished.

In this final chapter we'll look at the many blessing moments in *Gilead*. We'll ask what is meant by "blessing," then look at blessings in the Bible and in the novel, including the many baptisms.

What Is a Blessing?

> When my father found his father at Mount Pleasant after the war ended, he was shocked at first to see how he had been wounded. In fact, he was speechless. So my grandfather's first words to his son were "I am confident that I will find great blessing in it." And that is what he said about everything that happened to him for the rest of his life, all of which tended to be more or less drastic. I remember at least two sprained wrists and a cracked rib. (*Gilead*, 35–36)

We might take the grandfather's remark to mean that one must look for a "silver lining" in all of life's difficult situations. Sometimes we talk about taking the lemons of life and making lemonade. When we talk about blessing someone, we might understand this to be good wishes, happy thoughts, or positive energy.

We may understand "blessing" and what it is to "bless" someone or something in many different ways. In a religious service, a blessing—such as a benediction at the close of a service—might be a charge for the congregation to go forth to do God's work. Or it might be an expression of God's love and protection. In a wedding, it is a pronouncement of, or request for, God's favor. A parent's blessing to a child might be a request that he or she be prosperous or bear healthy children.

Old Testament scholar Walter Brueggemann defines blessing as "an act—by speech or gesture—whereby one party transmits power of life to another party" (*Reverberations of Faith,* Louisville: Westminster John Knox Press, 2002, p. 18). This is a very broad definition. Yet, "the power of life" encompasses a range of things from material wealth to life itself. Agents of blessing are either human or Divine. What does it mean to "transmit the power of life?"

Calling down God's gifts, such as children, material wealth, health, or professional success, on those we love or honor. In the Bible, human blessings do, indeed, hold the power to convey prosperous ends, even though God is the recognized source of the gifts. Recall from chapter 2 the story of Jacob, who tricked his father, Isaac, into bestowing his deathbed blessing on him.

Pronouncement of God's special favor. In the Magnificat (Lk. 1:46–55), Mary declared, "Surely, from now on all generations will call me blessed..."

Approval or sanction by God. While Ames lamented his poverty, he recognized that the "Lord Himself blessed [poverty] by word and example" (31).

Expressing, affirming, or acknowledging God's love. Affirming a person's place in God's world. When Ames asked God's blessing on the troubled Jack, he called him "this beloved son and brother and husband and father." The utterance of those familial roles in a sense restored Jack to those roles: "...to him it might have seemed I had named everything I thought he no longer was" (241).

Affirming the sacredness of a person or a situation. This was Ames's view of baptism (23, 91). He believed that a blessing did not make a person holy or sacred, but that through a blessing, God's gift of such sacredness was acknowledged.

Bringing of holiness to a situation that is not, in itself, a religious occasion, such as an illness or a new job. Blessings can be bestowed on objects, such as a new home, or a loaf of bread that will serve as communion. We might also think of "consecration," which is the setting aside of a person, place, or occasion for divine purpose.

Asking for God's protection, accompaniment, or anointing. We can ask that God be with someone about to undertake a journey, about to preach a sermon, or about to give birth.

Expressing thanks and praise to God. When we "bless God," we are expressing our desire to return the power of life to the very source of life.

Generally, then, blessing involves a special bestowal by God of a gift, whether the one doing the blessing is God or a person.

When you consider a friend to be a blessing to your life, you believe that God has given you a gift of this friend. When we believe a material object, such as a car, is a blessing, we acknowledge that the car is a gift from God, as are whatever abilities or earning powers enabled us to purchase it. When an experience turns out to be a blessing, such as Ames's trip to Kansas or the grandfather's sprained wrist, we believe God was at work for the good in that experience. When we bless a meal, we acknowledge God as the source of the sustenance and ask that its benefits be used for God's purpose. When we bless someone or something, we ask that it be a recipient of or vehicle for God's grace.

However we understand "blessing," we should be aware that the key component is God's participation. A "blessing" is not simply a good thing, positive coincidence, serendipity, or good wish. It is not luck or good fortune. A blessing involves an approval and a divine will that lay beyond the bounds of humankind.

Blessings (and Curses) in the Bible

The Bible's first chapter reports that the first thing God did after creating human beings was to bless them (Gen. 1:28). And, like many Old Testament blessings, God's blessing for humanity included successful and abundant procreation, control over the environment, and sustaining resources.

In the Bible, blessings come from both God and people. In the Old Testament, these blessings are generally for health, fertility, long life, and material wealth. In the New Testament, we find Jesus' pronouncement of blessing on certain behaviors, conditions, and attitudes. "Blessed are the poor in spirit…Blessed are those who mourn…Blessed are the meek…" (Mt. 5:1–12). The letters of Paul contain a number of blessings.

But the story of Bible blessings is not all sunshine and roses. Especially in the Old Testament, careful readers will note that blessings are often countered with curses.

Blessings in the Old Testament

It wasn't long after God blessed the new creatures called human beings that they incurred a curse (Gen. 3:16–19) and were kicked out of the garden of Eden. Their son Cain was also cursed (4:11). Because of humankind's "wickedness" (Gen. 6:5), God decided to destroy humankind with a flood, leaving only the righteous Noah and his family, whom God blessed (9:1). After Noah, God again cursed humanity, scattering all nations and confusing their language, in connection with humanity's building of the tower of Babel (Gen. 11).

But then the very significant blessing of Abraham conveyed to the patriarch land, progeny, and earthly prosperity and opened a new chapter in humankind's relationship with God:

> Now the LORD said to Abram, "Go from your country and your kindred and your father's house to the land that I will show you. I will make of you a great nation, and I will bless you, and make your name great, so that you will be a blessing. I will bless those who bless you, and the one who

> curses you I will curse; and in you all the families of the earth shall be blessed." (Gen. 12:1–3)

Note how the blessing itself contained a curse. Blessings and curses occur in tandem in the Old Testament. As Moses set the law before the Hebrew people in Deuteronomy, he said that those who obey and love God would be blessed; those who disobey the law and turn from God would be cursed (see Deut. 30). The history of the Hebrew people that followed (Josh. to 2 Kings) bore this out. When the people obeyed God, they were blessed; when they turned from God, disobeyed God, or paid homage to other gods, they suffered. The books of the prophets, too, carry these blessing-curse patterns.

Also note in God's blessing to Abraham that Abraham and the nation Israel were to be a blessing to humankind (see also Gen. 18:18). In the Old Testament, God's blessing was often mediated through people. Besides the nation Israel being a blessing, priests were known to be special vessels for God's life-giving power. The blessing that introduced this chapter is God's blessing that priests were to pronounce over the congregation. When Hannah went to the temple to pray for a child, the priest Eli assured her that her prayer would be granted (1 Sam. 1:9–17). A priestly blessing is more than a good wish; a priest's blessing carries within itself an assurance that it will be accomplished.

Other individuals are also bearers of God's blessing. Recall again Isaac's deathbed blessing in Genesis, and the power and promise it contained (Gen. 27:27–29). So desired was such a deathbed blessing, that Isaac's younger son, Jacob, resorted to an elaborate disguise to secure it for himself. So powerful was such a blessing that it functioned beyond Isaac's intention but could not be taken back or duplicated. When Esau discovered what had happened, he wept bitterly: "Esau said to his father, 'Have you only one blessing, father? Bless me, me also, father!" (Gen. 27:38).

Like other Old Testament blessings, Isaac's blessing of Jacob included dominion and material success. Blessings such as Isaac's could determine the destiny of the recipient. For other Old Testament blessings, see Jacob's blessing of Joseph's sons (Gen. 48:8–20) and Jacob's deathbed blessings of his twelve sons in Genesis 49:1–28. The blessing to each tribe describes its character and also predicts the future of each tribe. See also Rebekah's blessing in Genesis 24:60; Isaac's blessing in Genesis 26:2–4; Jacob's blessing in Genesis 32:29; and numerous human blessings of God in the book of Psalms, such as Psalms 128:5; 16:7; and 134.

Blessings in the New Testament

New Testament blessings also bestowed life. Jesus' pronouncement of God's favor and anticipated blessings can be found in the Beatitudes in Matthew 5:1–11 and in Luke 6:20–23. These "blessed are" statements are also in the Old Testament as in Psalm 1. They praised certain conditions or attitudes. Matthew and Luke emphasized different things. Note, for example, that Luke praised the poor and the hungry. Matthew, however, praised people who are "poor in spirit" and "hungry for righteousness." We can find other of these statements involving blessing in Romans 14:22; John 13:17; James 1:12; 1 Peter 3:14; Revelation 16:15.

Jesus also blessed meals. While the words Jesus may have uttered over the meals have been lost to us, it was his custom to bless food. In feeding the five thousand (Mt. 14:15–21; Lk. 9:12–17), Jesus took the five loaves and two fish, looked to heaven, blessed the loaves, broke them, and gave them to the disciples (see also Mk. 8:1–9). He again took bread, blessed it, broke, it and gave it to his disciples at the Last Supper (Mt. 26:26; Lk. 22:14–19).

Jesus blessed children by laying "his hands upon them" and by taking them in his arms (Mk. 10:16). His last earthly act before ascending into heaven was to bless the disciples (Lk. 24:50–51). Jesus instructed his followers to bless others, even their enemies, but not to curse (Lk. 6:28).

Except for a few places, the apostle Paul didn't use the word *blessed,* but many of his letters opened with a blessing of God: "Blessed be the God and Father of our Lord Jesus Christ, who has blessed us in Christ with every spiritual blessing…" (Eph. 1:3; see also Rom. 1:25). We might also understand Paul's typical opening of this letter: "Grace to you and peace" to be a blessing as it would bestow gifts of God, grace and peace, to the letter's recipients. For Paul, the communion cup was a "cup of blessing" (1 Cor. 10:16).

Blessings in Gilead

Through generations of hardship, the Ames ministers were positioned between the mysteries of Almighty God and the small-town Congregationalist flock of Gilead. It was their job to discern the hand of God in war, poverty, hunger, depression, illness, and death, and then to communicate that to a congregation. In other words, they had to recognize and point out the blessings.

It's not surprising that blessing moments form the foundation and structure of *Gilead.* Understanding both baptism and communion as blessings, we see how Ames's life in Gilead was punctuated with blessings: The baptisms of his daughter, his wife, his namesake; the communion offered to him by his father in the form of an ashy biscuit; and the communion he offered to his son. Ames persistently wished to lay his hand once again on Jack's brow to utter a blessing, and the fulfillment of that wish forms the climax of the novel.

Recall how the Old Testament blessings were often accompanied by curses. As we review the blessing moments in the novel, note how each was accompanied by a tone of sadness.

Ames's Blessing of Jack

Ames wrote to his son of many regrets and tensions in his life. We've discussed a number of these in previous chapters. One of his biggest and most troubling regrets was his ambivalence about this namesake, Jack. That ambivalence included his pent-up hostility toward his godson, his less-than-enthusiastic christening of him, his inability to understand or forgive him, and his desire to somehow bless Jack again.

Ames wrote: "I wish I could put my hand on his brow and calm away all the guilt and regret that is exaggerated or misplaced, or beyond rectification in terms of this world. Then I could see what I'm actually dealing with" (201).

Ames's vexation was twofold. First, he didn't like or understand his own heart about the boy. At Jack's baptism, Ames was shocked that the boy was to bear his name. His instinct was to deny any relationship with the baby, a sentiment he had not felt previously. "I remember the moment very clearly, Boughton and Mrs. Boughton and all the little ones there at the font, watching to see my joyful surprise, which I hope they did see, because my feelings at the time were a little more complex than I'd have wished" (155). Second, Ames didn't understand Jack's heart. He didn't understand him as a boy, an adolescent, or a young man. He remained suspicious of the middle-aged Jack, and hesitated to accept him as sincere or honest.

Recall from chapter 2 Ames's reconciliation with Jack on learning of Jack's family in Tennessee, and his sudden and deep identification with Jack over the unavailability to him of his wife and child. As the two men walked to the bus stop at the end of the novel, Ames was able to bestow on his godson the gifts of a book, and a more meaty discussion about salvation. He gave him money. "Then I said, 'The thing I would like, actually, is to bless you" (141).

This blessing was far more tender than the first, acknowledging all that Jack was, rather than insisting what Jack was not. It was a long-delayed gift to Boughton. And, it was a crucial moment in

Ames's ministry. Not only did it signal the bestowal of God's grace on Jack, but also the resolution of Ames's struggle to reconcile his human impulses as a man with his calling and duty as a minister.

Baptism and Naming

Among Ames's most cherished memories of ministry were the baptisms. As a child, he even baptized a litter of kittens. The baptism of Lila was a poignant instance, a mixture of sadness and beauty, as we recall from chapter 5.

In Ames's Congregationalist tradition, people are typically baptized as infants, with water being placed on their foreheads (sometimes called "sprinkling"). These aren't simply baptisms, but "christenings," in which the infant is ceremoniously named. These moments were precious for Ames, but he also appreciated the Baptists' practice of full immersion baptism, in which an older child or an adult is fully dunked under water:

> When I was in seminary I used to go sometimes to watch the Baptists down at the river. It was something to see the preacher lifting the one who was being baptized up out of the water and the water pouring off the garments and the hair. It did look like a birth or a resurrection. For us the water just heightens the touch of the pastor's hand on the sweet bones of the head, sort of like making an electrical connection. I've always loved to baptize people, though I have sometimes wished there were more shimmer and splash involved in the way we go about it. (*Gilead*, 63)

Whether by immersion or sprinkling, baptism is the sacrament through which a person is brought into the Christian church universal. Christians have brought other believers into the fold via baptism since the beginning of the church, and baptisms "in the name of the Father, Son, and Holy Ghost" have been practiced since at least the first century. For the apostle Paul, baptism indicated union with Christ. Baptism is also associated with forgiveness, new life, repentance, and receiving the Holy Spirit.

The first of many baptism moments that Ames recalled in his letter to his son was that of his daughter. She was born six weeks premature, while Ames was out of town (18). Because the girl was expected to die, Boughton officiated at the baptism. Ames, however, did have the opportunity to bless her: "I laid my hand on her just to bless her, and I could feel her pulse, her warmth, the damp of her hair" (56).

Boughton named the girl Angeline, from Matthew 18:10. Angeline, Ames wrote, is a "good name." Yet more often he referred to his child as Rebecca, the name he and his wife had picked out for her. This is another instance of an unexpected name coming at a christening, just as Jack's did.

Just as a blessing conveyed power in the Old Testament, so a person's name had power and meaning and could even influence his or her fortune. Recall how God bestowed new names on both Abram and Jacob (see chapter 2). *Jacob* means "he takes by the heel" or "he supplants." But as Jacob gets ready to meet the brother he tricked repeatedly, God gives him the name *Israel,* which means "he who strives with God" or "God strives." *Abram* means "exalted father," while *Abraham* means "father of a multitude." Abraham's abundant progeny is a key component in understanding God's relationship with the Hebrew people.

Although John Ames Boughton carried the names of ministers, he was called "Jack" and did not become a minister. While Rebecca's biblical namesake grew to maturity, married Isaac, and bore children to continue the patriarchal line, no such destiny awaited Ames's daughter. She was given a more angelic name, as she was destined to see the face of God in heaven.

Note how two children in *Gilead* are not named: Jack's little girl who died as a small child and Ames's son, whose future lies as a mystery before him. Perhaps by not giving Jack's daughter a name, Robinson hoped to convey her utter lack of future or that her parents did not claim or care for her. By not revealing the name of Ames's son, we are encouraged to guess at his future.

For Ames, baptism was an important form of blessing. Even baptizing the litter of kittens was important, not just for the future of their furry little souls, but by the very nature of blessing God's creatures: "I still remember how those warm little brows felt under the palm of my hand. Everyone has petted a cat, but to touch one like that with the pure intention of blessing it, is a very different thing" (23).

Ames acknowledged that in the baptism moment, he was not simply the bestower of blessing, but a receiver of blessing too. "whenever I take a child into my arms to be baptized, I am, so to speak, comprehended in the experience more fully, having seen more of life, knowing better what it means to affirm the sacredness of the human creature" (91).

Much of Ames's regret about his christening of Jack was that he didn't feel the holiness of the moment: "I do wish I could christen him again, for my sake. I was so distracted by my own miserable thoughts I didn't feel that sacredness under my hand that I always do feel, that sense that the infant is blessing me. Now that is a pity" (189).

Indeed, we are blessed when we bless others. But the primary actor in any blessing is God. Issuing a blessing to someone is not "about us." It's about conveying or acknowledging the life-giving power of God. As Martin Luther said about baptism:

> Hence we ought to understand baptism at human hands just as if Christ Himself, nay God Himself, baptized us with His own Hands. The baptism which we receive through human hands is Christ's and God's, just as everything else that we receive through human hands is God's. Be careful therefore, in regard to baptism, to ascribe only the external right to man, but the internal operation to God. (*Martin Luther, Selections from His Writings,* ed. John Dillenberger, New York: Doubleday, 1962, p. 296f)

Besides the official acts of baptism, christening, and blessing, Robinson also gives us several other "baptism moments." In a number of scenes, refreshment and renewal involve the interplay of humans and water. Recall how Ames was captured by the scene of his son and his son's friend Tobias playing in the sprinkler (63); the rain during the cleanup of the church fire (102–3); Edward's pouring water over his head as he plays catch, recalling the blessing of Aaron (64); the couple strolling under wet trees after a rain: "It was a beautiful thing to see, like something from a myth. I don't know why I thought of that now, except perhaps it is easy to believe in such moments that water was made primarily for blessing, and only secondarily for growing vegetables or doing the wash" (28).

Communion

Baptism is but one sacrament in the rich and varied tradition of the church. A sacrament is a means by which God expresses grace. A common definition is "an outward sign of an inward (or invisible) grace." The Roman Catholic Church understands there to be seven sacraments. Most Protestant denominations understand that Jesus gave his followers two: baptism and the Lord's supper, also called "communion" or "eucharist." *Gilead* contains two special eucharistic moments: when the Rev. John Ames II feeds his son the ashy biscuit at the site of the church fire, and when Ames gives his son communion.

Jesus instituted communion during the Last Supper on the night he was betrayed, when he gathered with his followers in an upper room (see Mt. 26:26–29; Mk. 14:22–25; Lk. 22:15–20; and 1 Cor. 11:23–25). In breaking the bread and sharing the cup, Jesus instructed his followers to "do this in remembrance of me." The word translated "remembrance" is a word that means more than a cognitive recollection, but a recollection so powerful that an actual presence of the absent person is experienced.

Many people find great comfort in the Lord's supper and experience a life-giving connection with God. Yet Ames associated the Lord's supper with sorrow. "Grief itself has often returned me to that morning, when I took communion from my father's hand. I remember it as communion, and I believe that's what it was" (63). Later, Ames described the celebration of the Lord's supper as "a time with the Lord in Gethsemane" (114, see chapter two).

Perhaps for Ames, communion symbolized the Christian understanding of the mysterious and paradoxical interplay of life and death. That understanding is connected to Jesus' death on Good Friday, which made possible his resurrection on Easter. Christians widely—but not unanimously—understand that Jesus' death was also necessary for God's people through the ages to hope for eternal life.

Ames often returned in his mind to that rainy day after the Baptist church burned. A bolt of lightning utterly destroyed hymnals, Bibles, walls, and pews. Yet the cleanup was a celebration. Grown women sang hymns and let their hair fall down their backs like schoolgirls. Children played marbles under wagons. Women brought pies and cakes, as older boys and men tore down what remained standing. In the midst of drought, no one minded the rain.

> My father brought me some biscuit that had soot on it from his hands. "Never mind," he said, "there's nothing cleaner than ash." But it affected the taste of that biscuit, which I thought might resemble the bread of affliction, which was often mentioned in those days, though it's rather forgotten now. (*Gilead*, 95)

Ames's memory was vivid, yet distorted to emphasize the eucharistic elements of the biscuit. He recalled that his father broke the bread and put a bit of it in his mouth; at the same time, he knew his father simply handed him half the biscuit. Ames further recalled that his father took "that bread from his side" (103) perhaps a reference to Jesus' side, which was pierced during the crucifixion and from which flowed water and blood (Jn. 19:34).

The memory of that day was so meaningful to Ames that he wished to convey part of that memory to his son. In Ames's church, the boy was too young to take communion. But after the service, Lila brought the boy forward, and Ames fed him a piece of bread and the cup.

> Your solemn and beautiful child face lifted up to receive these mysteries at my hands. They are the most wonderful mystery, body and blood.
>
> It was an experience I might have missed. Now I only fear I will not have time enough to fully enjoy the thought of it. (*Gilead*, 70)

Other Blessings

During the cleanup of the church fire, the people gathered up all the hymnals and Bibles that had been ruined. They dug holes in which to bury them. Importantly, Ames called the holes "graves."

The scene might call to mind another instance of burial of inanimate objects. Ames II attempted to erase part of his father by burying his pistol and other effects: "These things my grandfather had left were just an offense to him. So he buried them" (79). The hole Ames II dug was large, but apparently not large enough to contain his feelings about his father's pistol. A month later, Ames II dug the pistol up again, smashed it, and threw it into the river.

Note the differences in the way that Ames II handled the pistol, and the way the Baptist congregation handled the Bibles and hymnals. In the latter case, by having Ames call the holes "graves," Robinson encourages us to think of the books' burial as a funeral. A minister even offered a prayer over the books. A funeral is a blessing ceremony; burying the books so carefully acknowledged their sacredness and usefulness in praising God. Contrast this with Ames II's burial of the pistol. He did not bless the pistol. He cursed the item because it represented war, which Ames II abhorred. His wife, however, conferred blessing on the pistol's owner by caring for the grandfather's shirts so carefully before she buried them.

Ames described many events of his life as blessings. These included holding his infant daughter; the timely and convenient death of Lacey Thrush; his trip to Kansas; the fact that lightning struck the Baptist church on a Tuesday night; Glory's divorce; and the long period of loneliness before Lila entered his life.

Ames recalled with awe the phenomenon of the sun and the moon hovering on either side of the Kansas horizon. "Each of them was standing on its edge, with the most wonderful light between them. It seemed as if you could touch it, as if there were palpable currents of light passing back and forth, or as if there were great taut skeins of light suspended between them" (14). For the young Ames, it was a miracle, a "particular blessing my father had brought down by praying there at his father's grave, or the glory that my grandfather had somehow emanated out of his parched repose" (48).

Looking up from his prayer, Ames II also acknowledged the beauty of the scene. Later, walking in the moonlight, he denied the special nature of what they had witnessed. "He never encouraged any talk about visions or miracles, except the ones in the Bible" (48).

Blessings All Around Us

We might chuckle at the old grandfather's insistence on finding blessing in hard circumstances. We probably know people who reach far to find something to smile about. Indeed, these dubious "Pollyanna" types who always look for a silver lining might annoy us greatly. Sometimes life is difficult and passing over the difficulties too blithely can lead to a shallowness of life. Ignoring life's traumas and pressures can be irresponsible and merely postpone—and compound—the inevitable.

On the other hand, even worse than the perpetual Pollyanna is the perpetual pessimist who expects the worst. For this person, good things that happen are always merely a prelude to a terrible occurrence. As a boy, Ames saw a miracle in the alignment of sun and moon. His father preferred to be blind to such beauty as a manifestation of God's glory. To which Ames minister would you take your troubles?

We can learn a lesson from the old grandfather. Believing that all of life carries the potential for divine good puts us in a mind-set to recognize blessings as they occur. Whether or not we believe in God or ascribe to a certain faith, we can understand that life is generally good and worthwhile, that every person and situation carries goodness within it.

As we count our blessings, we should be mindful of those people who have little, who are oppressed, or who are stricken with addiction or disease. Esau's cry to his father should haunt us: "Have you not reserved a blessing for me?" God does not withhold blessings from us, but sometimes society does. In conveying God's blessings to people, Ames himself felt blessed. The point of blessing others is not to make us feel good, but we can appreciate how spreading God's life-giving power magnifies our own supply.

We can condition ourselves to look for blessings in the world around us. We can acknowledge the sacredness of events, people, and things by naming them as "blessings." And, we can act as agents of blessings by acknowledging the sacredness of fellow human beings, asking for God's mercy and protection over the vulnerable, reminding others of their sacredness, and always giving thanks to God. In becoming proclaimers of God's blessings, we can help bring about the reality of their abundance.

QUESTIONS FOR DISCUSSION

1. A number of times, Ames hinted at his curiosity about whether his son would be a minister (for example, p. 23). Can you predict how Robinson envisions the boy's future? He turned seven in the mid-1950s; calculate the point in history at which he will become an adult.
2. If a blessing is somehow a power to "give life," how can we "give life" to one another?
3. What do you think of Ames's blessing of Jack? Was it a catharsis? Should he, as a minister, have been able to bless Jack regardless of his feelings and suspicions? Why or why not?
4. Recall the scenes of the burned-down church, the "ashy biscuit," and the women dancing in the rain with their hair undone. Ames wrote "much of my life was comprehended in that moment" (96). What does he mean? What do you think the biscuit symbolizes? the burned church? the fact that the pulpit remained intact?

For Further Reading

Frederick Buechner, *Beyond Words: Daily Readings in the ABCs of Faith*. New York: Harper SanFrancisco, 2004.

Anne Lamott, *Traveling Mercies: Some Thoughts on Faith*. New York: Pantheon Books, 1999.

Henri J.M. Nouwen, *Bread for the Journey: A Day Book of Wisdom and Faith*. San Francisco: Harper SanFrancisco, 1997.

Keith Watkins, ed., *Baptism and Belonging*. St. Louis: Chalice Press, 1991.

CONCLUSION

There is a balm in Gilead
to make the wounded whole,
there is a balm in Gilead
to heal the sin-sick soul.

We opened this guide to the novel *Gilead* with a hymn that considers the fleeting nature of earthly time. We close also with a hymn, the old spiritual "There Is a Balm in Gilead." As we opened with a reflection on time, we think it fitting to close with a reflection on place: the small town of Gilead, Iowa.

For just as the issue of dwindling time formed a patina over the mood of *Gilead*, so the constancy of place provided a foundation on which were built the lives and loves of the Ames ministers, their families, their friends, and their flocks. Gilead was home to much pain and much sorrow. Was a soothing balm there as well?

The words of the African American spiritual come from Jeremiah 8:22: "Is there no balm in Gilead? / Is there no physician there? / Why then has the health of my poor people / not been restored?" The scripture asks the question. The hymn answers it: Indeed, there *is* a balm in Gilead, a balm that makes the wounded whole and heals the sin-sick soul.

Now we pose the question to the novel: Did the town of Gilead "make the wounded whole?" Almost every character in the novel bore a wound of some type: Old John Ames I bore the wounds of war; his son bore the wounds of poor relations with his father; Ames III bore the wounds of a lost wife and daughter, and also a brother and father who were in many ways lost to him. Lila's spirit was wounded that rainy day when she stepped into the church. Boughton bore the wounds of shame and unrequited hope for his son Jack. We believe that Gilead provided these last two with wholeness of spirit and wholeness of family.

As we leave our narrator to his prayer and his sleep, not much has changed since the beginning of the novel. His son still faces life without his father; Lila is left with stacks of sermons, but no financial savings. Boughton is still dying; the church still needs a new roof. Jack's relationship with his family is still troubled; his journey to find a home for his son and wife remains incomplete.

When the novel opened, we sensed Ames's restlessness: There was so much to do as his time on Earth melted away. The boxes of sermons had to be dealt with, the files in the church office had to be sorted. There were stories to tell his son, advice to give. The troubled relationship with Jack Boughton weighed heavy on his failing heart. Ames always appreciated the beauty and blessings of life, but it was as if he hadn't appreciated them deeply enough. In his final days, he found that water was far more exquisite than he had understood. People were far more beautiful; the simple act of catching a baseball was a miraculous coordination of muscle, bone, and mind.

By the end of the novel, however, restlessness has given way to peace. Anxiety has given way to stillness. Death has become no longer a deadline, but a continuation of life. We believe that, yes, in the case of the Rev. John Ames III, the small town of Gilead, Iowa, has indeed made the wounded whole.

Did the balm in Gilead also heal the sin-sick soul? To answer this question, we look at Jack Boughton, for whom that description seems most apt. When Jack arrived about one-third of the way through the novel, much to the delight of his family and the fascination of Ames's wife and child, we already had an opinion about him. It was made no better by Ames's reaction to him. Jack was troubled, but were his troubles his own fault? He had been a thief, a cad, and a ne'er-do-well. Had he repented? Had he even felt remorse? He came to Ames seeking answers to age-old religious quandaries. Were his inquiries sincere, or was he just trying to stir things up? Just how dangerous was he? We recall through whose eyes we are experiencing this story.

Jack came to Gilead to lay down his sins, to lay bare his soul, and to find healing for the difficult life ahead of him. His biggest obstacle was healing his relationship with Ames, who himself anguished over his inability to forgive his godson. Ultimately, we believe the two reconciled and connected on a very deep level, man-to-man, son-to-son, father-to-father, and pilgrim-to-pilgrim. In this respect, we believe Jack's sin-sick soul was healed. We believe it was healed in the courageous admission of his secret family. We believe it was healed in his persistence in trying to connect with Ames. We believe it was healed in his expressions of love and friendliness, and in the love, acceptance, and even blessing he found in the arms of his family, and in Ames's family.

Healing, however, does not mean cure. For while the town of Gilead provided a balm of healing and wholeness, it was not the final destiny of all who dwelled there. We lift up three other characters who did not, in the end, make Gilead their final home: Ames I, Ames II, and Edward. We spoke much about the parable of the prodigal son. A key part of that story is the younger son's return to his father, and his father's eager embrace of him. As we hold the *Gilead* men to this standard, we note two things.

First, while people return to Gilead, they don't always stay. We should not understand this as a failure on the part of those who ultimately leave, of their families, or of the town. Nor are these necessarily missed opportunities at resolution, for resolution does not always mean "yes." Ames I came to Gilead, tried to revive a dying church and live with a pacifist son and his practical wife. In the end, he returned to Kansas, the place where perhaps he found his greatest satisfaction in life.

Second, as human beings we are composites of complex feelings that make our high ideals of behavior almost impossible to achieve. Ames III's and Glory's feelings about Jack included their memories of his past failings, suspicions about his motivations, and deep concern about Boughton. As a minister, Ames in particular may have wanted in his heart to open his arms to his godson with unreserved acceptance—like the father of the prodigal son—but he could not erase his ambivalent feelings and negative memories.

If we understand the father in Luke's parable to represent God, we can rest in the blessing of God's acceptance of those who have failed, strayed, sinned, and made foolish decisions. God's acceptance and human acceptance are two different things, for God can see into our souls in ways that even those who love us the most cannot. We shouldn't be too hard on Ames for resisting acceptance of his godson. We can, however, marvel and rejoice at his change of heart.

Some questions linger for us: What is the climax of the novel? When Jack tells Ames the story of his wife and son? Ames's blessing at the bus station? Is everything ultimately resolved? Did Ames forgive Jack? Was it his place to forgive him? What will become of Lila and the unnamed boy?

If you have read Gilead one time through, we leave you with an encouragement to read it again. We expect you will find the themes more profound, the pain more anguished, the joy more cherished. Is there a balm in Gilead? Because of the richness and depth of Robinson's characters, we believe that question is ultimately to be answered by you, the reader.

We conclude with Ames's final thoughts on his hometown, a place of birth and death, hunger and plenty, sorrow and joy, beauty and hardship:

> This whole town does look like whatever hope becomes after it begins to weary a little, then weary a little more. But hope deferred is still hope. I love this town. I think sometimes of going into the ground here as a last wild gesture of love—I too will smolder away the time until the great and general incandescence (*Gilead,* 247).